Sweet Baby Crochet

20 Crochet Patterns for Girls & Boys Newborn to 24 Months

Sandy Powers | Photography by Tara Renaud

Published by **Sellers Publishing, Inc.**
161 John Roberts Road, South Portland, Maine 04106

Visit our Web site: www.sellerspublishing.com
E-mail: rsp@rsvp.com

Design and layout copyright © 2016 BlueRed Press Ltd
Text copyright © 2016 Sandy Powers
Patterns copyright © 2016 Sandy Powers
Photography by Tara Renaud
All rights reserved.
Design by Insight Design Concepts Ltd.

ISBN 13: 978-1-4162-4581-0
Library of Congress Number 2015946620

10 9 8 7 6 5 4 3 2 1

Printed and bound in China

Contents

SKILL LEVEL – easy

SKILL LEVEL – intermediate

SKILL LEVEL – easy to intermediate

CROCHET HOOK SIZES

METRIC SIZES (mm)	US SIZES	UK / CANADIAN
2.0	-	14
2.25	B/1	13
2.5	-	12
2.75	C/2	-
3.0	-	11
3.25	D/3	10
3.5	E/4	9
3.75	F/5	-
4.0	G/6	8
4.5	7	7
5.0	H/8	6
5.5	I/9	5
6.0	J/10	4
6.5	K/10 ½	3
7.0	-	2
8.0	L/11	0
9.0	M/13	00
10.0	N/15	000

Crochet Essentials

Magic Circle instructions

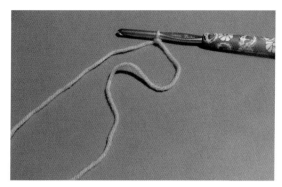

Step 1 make a slip knot on the crochet hook, leaving a long starting tail to work with.

Step 2 with the long starting tail, loop around the fingers.

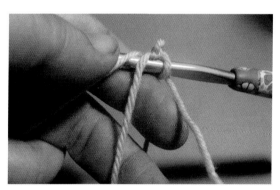

Step 3 yarn over and bring the yarn back through the loop on the fingers.

Step 4 1 st sc made in a loop.

Step 5 pull the long straight tight to close the circle. Secure the tail with a knot.

Magic Circle technique is used in the following projects:

p. 6   Poncho and Hat Set
p. 68   Owl Afghan
p. 74   Owl Costume
p. 84   Owl Mobile
p. 116   Sweet Bonnet and Adorable Bear

NOTE: A hank is a long and twisted length of yarn that needs to be wound into a ball of yarn. You can't work with it until you wind it. A skein – or ball – is a yarn that can be worked from immediately.

Introduction

My name is Sandy Yurkins Powers, and as many of you already know, I love to design clothing and accessories for babies. Recently, I was inspired, and truly motivated, to create some new designs: our daughter Christina gave birth to her first child and our first grandchild, sweet baby Lily!

Now that you know the inspiration for my new book, *Sweet Baby Crochet*, I have to confess that it was hard some days to try to design something for boys when all I wanted to do was design for my granddaughter! Despite that, I've included a lot of patterns that can be made for both boys and girls. We had so much fun creating these designs and Lily often made an appearance to model the outfits. Tara Renaud, our photographer for the book, took many wonderful, cute, and memorable pictures of her this past year.

The designs in *Sweet Baby Crochet* include items for all seasons. The adorable fox and lamb coveralls will keep babies warm in spring and autumn, and the handsome Fisherman Vest is perfect for holiday occasions. The all-cotton rompers and the Sailor Suit are for those warm summer days, and the one-of-a kind designs such as the owl and the "lobstah" are charming outfits for baby pictures; likewise, the Princess Roses Tulle Dress, the Crowns, and the Bonnets and Bears. I've included three afghans for lots of cuddles and snuggles. And new moms will love using the Snail Diaper Bag, complete with diaper changing pad.

This book took me a lot longer to make than usual. Soon after I began *Sweet Baby Crochet*, I learned that I had bilateral breast cancer. I had two surgeries and two months of radiation, all while working on my patterns for this book. This book truly is my labor of love and I hope you will enjoy these crochet designs for years to come.

Poncho and Hat Set

More beautiful than the rose is the young lady wearing them. Embellished with one floret or a dozen, your little girl will look sweet and adorable in this stylish washable wool poncho and hat set. Suitable for a special occasion or a stroll in the park, it's the perfect ensemble for the star of your bouquet. Everything's coming up roses!

Yarn

Cascade 220 Superwash 3.5oz/100g/220yds/200m/ #4 medium weight

Colors used in pictures:

Color number 871 / Color name: White x 2 (2, 2, 3, 3) skeins

Color number 835 / Color name: Ice Pink Rose x 1 skein

Color number 851 / Color name: Lime x 1 skein

Needle

US I9/5.50mm Susan Bates hook

US H8/5.00mm Susan Bates hook

US G6/4.00mm Susan Bates hook

Yarn needle

Gauge

I Hook = 7dc rows x 13dc = 4"

Glossary of Abbreviations

rnd(s) = round(s)

FL = front loop(s)

BL = back loop(s)

ch = chain

chsp = chain space

sc = single crochet

slst = slip stitch

dc = double crochet

hdc = half double crochet

sk = skip

rep from * to* = repeat from between the stars

vshell = vshell- 2dc, ch2, 2 dc all in same ch space

vstitch = vst: 1dc, ch2, 1dc all in the same ch space

Finished Sizes

0–3 months, 3–6 months, 6–12 months, 12–18 months, 18–24 months

Instructions are written 0–3, other sizes are in parenthesis

Notes: Entire poncho is worked on the right side. Do not turn.

PONCHO

(Note: See Poncho and Hat Set stitches p. 11)

With I hook and White, ch 50 (50, 50, 60, 60). Being careful not to twist the chain, join to first ch. Ch 3. (See Fig 1 p. 11.)

Rnd 1: Do not turn, dc in the next 8ch, work (2dc, ch2, 2dc) all in the next ch, (shell made) 1dc in the next 24ch (24ch, 24ch, 29ch, 29ch), vshell in next ch, 1dc in each of the next 15ch (15ch, 15ch, 20ch, 20ch). Join with slst in top of ch3. (56dc, 56dc, 56dc, 66dc, 66dc). (See Fig 2 p. 11.)

Rnds 2–14 (2–16, 2–18, 2–20, 2–22): Ch3, 1dc in each dc to first ch2space, vshell in ch2space, 1dc each dc to the next ch2space, vshell in ch2space, 1dc in each dc to end of rnd. Slst to join rnd. Each rnd will increase by 8dc.

Rnd 15 (17, 19, 21, 23): Ch3, 1dc in the BL of each dc to first ch2space, vshell in ch2space, 1dc in the BL of each dc to next ch2space, vshell in ch2space, 1dc in the BL of each dc to end of rnd. Slst to join.

Rnds 16–17 (18–20, 20–23, 22–26, 24–29): Ch3, 1dc in each dc to first ch2space, vshell in ch2space, 1dc each dc to the next ch2space, vshell in ch2space, 1dc in each dc to end of rnd. Slst to join rnd.

Rnd 18 (21, 24, 27, 30): Ch1, 1sc in same st as joining, sk next sc, *6dc in next sc, sk next sc, 1slst in next sc, sk next sc*, rep from * to * around. Slst to join rnd. Fasten off and weave in ends.

Continue on to Lime Trim for all sizes

0–3 month hat 14" circumference 5" tall
Rnd 1: With H hook and White, make a magic circle (see p. 4), 12dc inside loop, pull loop tight. Slst to join. (12dc)

Rnd 2: Ch1, 2dc in same st as joining, 2dc in each dc around. Slst to join. (24dc)

Rnd 3: Ch1, 1dc in same st as joining, 2dc in next dc, *1dc in next dc, 2dc in next dc* rep from * to * around. Slst to join. (36dc).

Rnd 4–7: Ch1, 1dc in same st as joining, in each dc around. Slst to join. (36dc).

Rnds 8–9: Ch1, 1sc in same st as joining, 1sc in each st around. Slst to join. (36sc)

Rnd 10: Ch1, 1sc in the BL in the same st as joining, 1sc in the BL of each sc around. Slst to join. (36sc)

Rnd 11: Ch1, 2sc in same st as joining, 1sc in next sc, *2sc in next sc, 1sc in next sc* rep from * to * around. Slst to join.

Rnd 12: Ch1, 1sc in the same st as joining, 1sc in each sc around. Slst to join.

Rnd 13: Ch1, 1sc in same st as joining, sk next sc, 5dc in next sc, sk next sc, *1slst in next sc, sk next sc, 5dc in next sc, sk next sc* rep from * to * around. Slst to join. Fasten off and weave in ends.

Continue on to Lime Trim, work into FL that was created from the BL on rnd 10.

3–6 months 15" circumference 5" tall
Rnd 1: With H hook and White, make a magic circle (see p. 4), 12dc inside loop, pull loop tight. Slst to join. (12dc)

Rnd 2: Ch1, 2dc in same st as joining, 2dc in each dc around. Slst to join. (24dc)

Rnd 3: Ch1, 1dc in same st as joining, 2dc in next dc, *1dc in next dc, 2dc in next dc* rep from * to * around. Slst to join. (36dc).

Rnd 4: Ch1, 1dc in same st as joining, 1dc in next 3dc, 2dc in next dc, *1dc in next 4dc, 2dc in next dc* rep from * to * around. Slst to join. (42dc)

Rnds 5–8: Ch1, 1dc in same st as joining, 1dc in each dc around. Slst to join. (42dc)

Rnd 9–10: Ch1, 1sc in same st as joining, 1sc in each st around. Slst to join. (42sc)

Rnd 11: Ch1, 1sc in the BL of the same st as joining, 1sc in BL of each st around. Slst to join.

Rnd 12: Ch1, 2sc in same st as joining, 1sc in next sc, *2sc in next sc, 1sc in next sc* rep from * to * around. Slst to join.

Rnd 13: Ch1, 1sc in the same st as joining, 1sc in each st around. Slst to join.

Rnd 14: Ch1, 1sc in same st as joining, sk next sc, 5dc in next sc, sk next sc, *1slst in next sc, sk next sc, 5dc in next sc, sk next sc* rep from * to * around. Slst to join. Fasten off and weave in ends.

Continue on to Lime Trim, work into FL that was created from the BL on rnd 11.

6–12 months 16" circumference 5.5" tall

Rnd 1: With H hook and White, make a magic circle (see p. 4), 12dc inside loop, pull loop tight. Slst to join. (12dc)

Rnd 2: Ch1, 2dc in same st as joining, 2dc in each dc around. Slst to join. (24dc)

Rnd 3: Ch1, 1dc in same st as joining, 2dc in next dc, *1dc in next dc, 2dc in next dc* rep from * to * around. Slst to join. (36dc).

Rnd 4: Ch1, 1dc in same st as joining, 1dc in next dc, 2dc in next dc, *1dc in next 2dc, 2dc in next dc* rep from * to * around. Slst to join. (48dc)

Rnds 5–9: Ch1, 1dc in same st as joining, 1dc in each dc around. Slst to join. (48dc)

Rnds 10–11: Ch1, 1sc in same st as joining, 1sc in each st around. Slst to join. (48sc)

Rnd 12: Ch1, 1sc in the BL in the same st as joining, 1sc in the BL of each st around. Slst to join. (48sc)

Rnd 13: Ch1, 2sc in same st as joining, 1sc in next sc, *2sc in next sc, 1sc in next sc* rep from * to * around. Slst to join.

Rnd 14: Ch1, 1sc in the same st as joining, 1sc in the each st around. Slst to join.

Rnd 15: Ch1, 1sc in same st as joining, sk next sc, 5dc in next sc, sk next sc, *1slst in next sc, sk next sc, 5dc in next sc, sk next sc* rep from * to * around. Slst to join. Fasten off and weave in ends.

Continue on to Lime Trim, work in to FL that was created from the BL on rnd 12.

12–18 months 17" circumference 5.75" tall

Rnd 1: With H hook and White, make a magic circle (see p. 4), 12dc inside loop, pull loop tight. Slst to join. (12dc)

Rnd 2: Ch1, 2dc in same st as joining, 2dc in each dc around. Slst to join. (24dc)

Rnd 3: Ch1, 1dc in same st as joining, 2dc in next dc, *1dc in next dc, 2dc in next dc* rep from * to * around. Slst to join. (36dc).

Rnd 4: Ch1, 1dc in same st as joining, 1dc in next dc, 2dc in next dc, *1dc in next 2dc, 2dc in next dc* rep from * to * around. Slst to join. (48dc)

Rnd 5: Ch1, 1dc same st as joining, 1dc in next 6dc, 2dc in next dc *1dc in next 7dc, 2dc in next dc* rep from * to * around. Slst to join. (54dc)

Rnds 6–10: Ch1, 1dc in same st as joining, 1dc in each dc around. Slst to join. (54dc)

Rnd 11–12: Ch1, 1sc in same st as joining, 1sc in each dc around. Slst to join. (54sc)

Rnd 13: Ch1, 1sc in BL of the same st as joining, 1sc in BL of each st around. Slst to join. (54sc)

Rnd 14: Ch1, 2sc in same st as joining, 1sc in next sc, *2sc in next sc, 1sc in next sc* rep from * to * around. Slst to join.

Rnd 15: Ch1, 1sc in the same st as joining, 1sc in each st around. Slst to join.

Rnd 16: Ch1, 1sc in same st as joining, sk next sc, 5dc in next sc, sk next sc, *1slst in next sc, sk next sc, 5dc in next sc, sk next sc* rep from * to * around. Slst to join. Fasten off and weave in ends.

Continue onto Lime Trim, work into FL that was created from the BL on rnd 13

18–24 months 18" circumference 6" tall

Rnd 1: With H hook and White, make a magic circle (see p. 4), 12dc inside loop, pull loop tight. Slst to join. (12dc)

Rnd 2: Ch1, 2dc in same st as joining, 2dc in each dc around. Slst to join. (24dc)

Rnd 3: Ch1, 1dc in same st as joining, 2dc in next dc, *1dc in next dc, 2dc in next dc* rep from * to * around. Slst to join. (36dc).

Rnd 4: Ch1, 1dc in same st as joining, 1dc in next dc, 2dc in next dc, *1dc in next 2dc, 2dc in next dc* rep from * to * around. Slst to join. (48dc)

Rnd 5: Ch1, 1dc same st as joining, 1dc in next 2dc, 2dc in next dc *1dc in next 3dc, 2dc in next dc* rep from * to * around. Slst to join. (60dc)

Rnds 6–12: Ch1, 1dc in same st as joining, 1dc in each dc around. Slst to join. (60dc)

Rnd 13–14: Ch1, 1sc in same st as joining, 1sc in each dc around. Slst to join. (60sc)

Rnd 15: Ch1, 1sc in BL of same st as joining, 1sc in BL of each st around. Slst to join. (60sc)

Rnd 16: Ch1, 2sc in same st as joining, 1sc in next sc, *2sc in next sc, 1sc in next sc* rep from * to * around. Slst to join.

Rnd 17: Ch1, 1sc in the same st as joining, 1sc in each st around. Slst to join.

Rnd 18: Ch1, 1sc in same st as joining, sk next sc, 5dc in next sc, sk next sc, *1slst in next sc, sk next sc, 5dc in next sc, sk next sc* rep from * to * around. Slst to join. Fasten off and weave in ends.

Continue on to Lime Trim, work into FL that was created from the BL on rnd 15.

LIME TRIM FOR ALL HAT SIZES AND PONCHO

With top of hat facing you or neck opening facing you, and G hook, attach Lime to any FL that was created when you made the BL, ch1, 1sc in same st as joining, sk next st, *6sc in next st, sk next st, 1slst in next st, sk next st* repeat from * to * around. Slst to join rnd. Fasten off weave in ends. (See Fig 3 opposite.)

LIME TRIM FOR PONCHO NECK

Rnd 1: With neck opening facing you, attach Lime to any st on first rnd of neck, 1sc in each st around. Slst to join. (See Fig 3 opposite.)

Rnd 2: Ch1, 1sc in same st as joining, sk next st, *6sc in next st, sk next st, 1slst in next st, sk next st* repeat from * to * around. Slst to join rnd. Fasten off weave in ends.

ROSES

(Note: See Small Roses stitches p. 124)
make as many as desired for hat and poncho
Row 1: With G hook and Pink Ice, ch10, 2sc in 2nd ch from hook, 2sc in next 2ch, 2hdc in next 3ch, 3dc in next 3ch. Fasten off, leaving a tail to sew with. Roll stitches into a rose shape and draw some yarn through bottom of roll stitches to hold them into a rose shape. (See Figs 4–6 opposite.)

LEAVES

make as many as desired for hat and poncho

Rnd 1: With G hook and Lime ch6, 1sc in 2nd ch from hook, 1hdc in next ch, 1dc in next ch, 1hdc in next ch, 1sc in last ch, ch3, slst in 2nd ch from hook, 1sc in next ch, slst in top of sc. Now working on opposite side of leaf, 1hdc in next ch, 1dc in next ch, 1hdc in next ch, slst to first st to join. Fasten off, leaving a tail to sew with. Sew leaf onto bottom of roses. Sew roses and leaves onto lime trim in any desired places on hat and poncho. (See Fig 7 opposite.)

Poncho and Hat Set stitches

(Fig 1) slst to form circle for neck opening. (See p. 8.)

(Fig 2) neck. (See p. 8.)

(Fig 3) lime trim. (See p. 10.)

(Fig 4) make a rose. (See p. 10.)

(Fig 5) rolled rose with sc to close. (See p. 10.)

(Fig 6) sew rose on. (See p. 10.)

(Fig 7) row 3. Sew leaves on. (See p. 10.)

Sailor Suit

Land ahoy! It's a seafaring sailor suit for girls and boys! Batten down the hatches, this stylish nautical romper is made with cool, breathable cotton. Your adorable cadet will be comfortable on land or at sea.

Yarn

Cascade Ultra Pima Cotton 3.5oz/100g/220yds/209m/#3 lightweight cotton

Colors used in pictures:

Color number 3750 / Color name: Tangerine x 2 (2,3,3,3) hanks (MC)

Color number 3753 / Color name: White Peach x 1 (1,1,2,2) hank (CC)

Color number 3728 / Color name: White x 1 hank (stars)

Needle

US G6/4.00mm Susan Bates hook

Yarn Needle

Gauge

18sc x 22sc rows = 4"

Other Items

6 – ½" buttons

Glossary of Abbreviations

st(s) = stitch(es)	chsp = chain space
slst = slip stitch	ch = chain
beg = beginning	sc = single crochet
BL = Back loop(s)	dc = double crochet
sk = skip	hdc = half double crochet
rnd(s) = round(s)	MC = main color
rem = remaining	CC = contrasting color

CS = Corner Stitches: (1sc, ch3, 1sc) all in next st or chsp

Finished Sizes

0–3 months = approx 17" chest – shoulder to crotch approx 12"

3–6 months = approx 18" chest – shoulder to crotch approx 13"

6–12 months = approx 19" chest – shoulder to crotch approx 14"

12–18 months = approx 22" chest – shoulder to crotch approx 15"

18–24 months = approx 25" chest – shoulder to crotch approx 17"

Instructions are written 0–3, other sizes are in parenthesis

Sailor Suit stitches

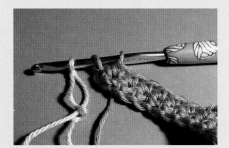

(Fig 1) change colors on bodice to start second stripe. (See Row 2.)

(Fig 2) yoke for bodice. (See opposite Row 7–10.)

(Fig 3) making armhole. (See opposite Row 1.)

(Fig 4) working in ends of rows to make buttonbands. (See opposite.)

(Fig 5) forming leg. (See First Leg Row 1, p. 16.)

(Fig 6) back flap of collar. (See Collar Rows 3–9 p. 16.)

(Fig 7) 5sc inside magic circle (see p. 4). (See Stars Rnd 1 p.16.)

(Fig 8) sew stars on the front and back in corners of collar. (See Stars 2nd–5th points p. 16.)

BODICE

Work all sizes to row 10.

Row 1: With G hook and MC, ch35 (ch39, ch42, ch45, ch48), 1sc in 2nd ch from hook, 1sc in each rem ch. Turn. 34sc (38sc, 41sc, 44sc, 47sc)

Row 2: Ch1, 1sc in next 5sc (6sc, 6sc, 7sc, 7sc), (1sc, ch3, 1sc all in next sc), 1sc in next 5sc (5sc, 6sc, 6sc, 7sc,), CS, 1sc in next 10sc (12sc, 13sc, 14sc, 14sc), CS, 1sc in next 5sc (5sc, 6sc, 6sc.7sc), CS, 1sc in next 5sc (6sc, 6sc, 7sc, 7sc). Turn. (38sc, 42sc, 5sc, 48sc, 50sc) change to CC, do not fasten off MC, just drop that color strand for now and pick it for every other row. (See Fig 1 opposite.)

Row 3: With CC, attach to first st, ch1, 1sc in next 6sc (7c, 7sc, 8sc, 8sc), CS, 1sc in next 7sc (7sc, 8sc, 8sc, 9sc), CS, 1sc in next 12sc (14sc, 15sc, 16sc, 16sc), CS, 1sc in next 7sc (7sc, 8sc, 8sc, 9sc), CS, 1sc in next 6sc (8sc, 7sc, 8sc, 8sc). Turn. (46sc, 50sc, 53sc, 56sc, 58sc)

Row 4: Ch1, 1sc in next 7sc (8sc, 8sc, 9sc, 9sc), CS, 1sc in next 9sc (9sc, 10sc, 10sc, 11sc), CS, 1sc in next 14sc (16sc, 17sc, 18sc, 18sc), CS, 1sc in next 9sc (9sc, 10sc, 10sc, 11sc), CS, 1sc in next 7sc (8sc, 8sc, 9sc, 9sc). Turn. (54sc, 58sc, 61sc, 64sc, 66sc) Change back to MC.

Row 5: With MC, ch1, 1sc in next 8sc (9sc, 9sc, 10sc, 10sc), CS, 1sc in next 11sc, (11sc, 12sc, 12sc, 13sc), CS, 1sc in next 16sc (18sc, 19sc, 20sc, 20sc), CS, 1sc in next 11sc (11sc, 12sc, 12sc, 13sc), CS, 1sc in next 8sc (9sc, 9sc, 10sc, 10sc). Turn. (62sc, 66sc, 69sc, 72sc, 74sc)

Row 6: Ch1, 1sc in next 9sc (10sc, 10sc, 11sc, 11sc), CS, 1sc in next 13sc (13sc, 14sc, 14sc, 15sc), CS, 1sc in next 18sc (20sc, 21sc, 22sc, 22sc), CS, 1sc in next 13sc (13sc, 14sc, 14sc, 15sc), CS, 1sc in next 9sc (10sc, 10sc, 11sc, 11sc). Turn. (70sc, 74sc, 77sc, 80sc, 82sc) Change to CC.

Rows 7–10 (7–10, 7–12, 7–14, 7–16): Work in established pattern, changing colors every other row as established for each size and increasing each row by 8sc. Each size will end with a different color. So just make sure to continue striping in established colors. 102sc (106sc, 125sc, 144sc, 170sc). (See Fig 2 opposite for last row of all sizes.)

Forming Armhole Openings

Row 1: Continue to keep striping correct as you work these next rows. Ch1, 1sc in next 14sc (15sc, 17sc, 20sc, 22sc), 1sc in next ch3sp, sk next 23sc (28sc, 28sc, 32sc, 37sc), 1sc in next ch3sp, 1sc in next 28sc (30sc, 35sc, 41sc, 44sc), 1sc in next ch3sp, sk next 23sc (23sc, 28sc, 32sc, 37sc), 1sc in next ch3sp, 1sc in next 14sc (15sc, 17sc, 20sc, 22sc). Turn. 60sc (64sc, 73sc, 84sc, 92sc). (See Fig 3 opposite.)

Row 2: 1sc in each sc across. Turn. (60sc, 64sc, 73sc, 84sc, 91sc) Change color.

Rows 3–4: Ch1, 1sc in each sc across. Turn. (60sc, 64sc, 73sc, 84sc, 91sc) At end of rnd 4 change color.

Rows 5–6: Ch1, 1sc in each sc across. Turn. (60sc, 64sc, 73sc, 84sc, 91sc) At end of rnd 6 change color.

Rows 7–20 (7–22, 7–24, 7–28, 7–32): repeat rows 3–6 in sequence.

Fasten off White Peach and continue on to buttonbands with Tangerine.

BUTTONBANDS

For girls the button holes are on the right side.
For boys the button holes are on the left side.
All the suits in these pictures have the buttons holes on the left side.
To make a button hole just ch2 and sk next sc. Then next row, work only 1sc over the ch2sp, not 2sc.

Row 1: With Tangerine, working in ends of rows up right front side, 1sc in each end of row. Turn. (See Fig 4 opposite.)

Rows 2–3: Ch1, 1sc in each sc across. Turn.

Neck Edge
Row 1: 1sc in each st across neck edge over to left front side.

Left Band
Row 1: 1sc in ends of rows. Turn.

Row 2: Ch1, sc in each sc across adding buttonholes evenly spaced across and making as many as desired. Turn.

Row 3: Ch1, 1sc in each sc and in each ch across.

Next: overlap buttonhole band on top of buttonband. Working through both thicknesses, 1sc in each end of row in bottom of buttonbands, 1sc in each sc around. Do not slst to join rnd but continue working in a spiral. (62sc, 66sc, 76sc, 86sc, 94sc)

Lower body/top of shorts
Row 1: 1hdc in each sc around. Work in continuous rnds. (62hdc, 66hdc, 76hdc, 86hdc, 94hdc)

Row 2: 1hdc in between each hdc around. Work in continuous rnds. (62hdc, 66hdc, 76hdc, 86hdc, 94hdc)

Rows 3–10 (3–11, 3–13, 3–14, 3–15): 1hdc in between each hdc around. (62hdc, 66hdc, 76hdc, 86hdc, 94hdc)

First Leg

Row 1: Find the middle of the front of your shorts, insert hook into st opposite the beg st to form circle of first leg st, slst sts tog, ch1, 1hdc in between each hdc around. Slst to join rnd. (31hdc, 33hdc, 38hdc, 43hdc, 47hdc) (See Fig 5 on p. 14.)

Rows 2–6 (2–6, 2–7, 2–8, 2–9): Ch1, 1hdc in same st as joining, 1hdc in between each hdc around. Slst to join rnd. (31hdc, 33hdc, 38hdc, 43hdc, 47hdc) At end of last row fasten off and weave in ends.

Second Leg

Row 1: Attach MC to first hdc on 2nd leg, 1hdc in each hdc around. Slst to join. (31hdc, 33hdc,38hdc, 43hdc, 47hdc)

Rows 2–6 (2–6, 2–7, 2–8, 2–9): Ch1, 1hdc in same st as joining, 1hdc in each hdc around. Slst to join rnd. (31hdc, 33hdc, 38hdc, 43hdc, 47hdc) At end of last row fasten off and weave in ends.

Sleeves – make 2

Row 1: With MC, attach yarn to underarm opening. 1sc in each st around. Slst to join rnd. (24, 26s, 30sc.34sc, 40sc)

Rows 2–6 (2–7, 2–8, 2–9, 2–10): Ch1, 1sc in same st as joining, 1sc in each sc around. Slst to join. (24sc, 26sc, 30sc, 34sc, 40sc) At end of last row, fasten off and weave in ends.

Collar

Note: work row 1 only in BL.

Row 1: With MC, skipping the 1st 3 rows of buttonband, and with inside of suit facing you, attach MC to next st on neck edge, 1sc in next 5sc (6sc, 6sc, 7sc, 7sc), CS, 1sc in next 5sc (5sc, 6sc, 6sc, 7sc) CS, 1sc in next 10sc (12sc, 14sc, 14sc, 14dc) CS, 1sc in next 5sc (5sc, 6sc, 6sc, 7sc) CS, 1sc in next 5sc (6sc, 6sc, 7sc, 7sc)Turn. (38sc, 42sc, 46sc, 48sc, 50sc)

Row 2: Ch1, 1sc in next 6sc (7sc, 7sc, 8sc, 8sc) CS, in next 7sc (7sc, 8sc, 8sc, 9sc) CS, 1sc in next 12sc (14sc, 16sc, 16sc, 16sc), CS, 1sc in next 7sc (7sc, 8sc, 8sc, 9sc), CS, 1sc in next 6sc (7sc, 7sc, 8sc, 8sc) Turn. (46sc, 50sc, 54sc, 56sc, 58sc)

Rows 3–9 (3–10, 3–11, 13–12): Work in established pattern and increase 8sc every rnd. At end of last row, fasten off leaving a tail to sew with. Sew front corners to front of suit. (See Fig 6 on p. 14; this shows last rows on collars 9,10,11,12,13; add 3-13 for last size.)

Stars

make 5

Rnd 1: With G hook and White, make a magic circle (see p. 4), 5sc inside loop, pull loop tight. Slst to join. (5sc). (see Fig 7 on p. 14.)

1st point: ch3, 1slst in 2nd ch from hook, 1sc in next ch, 1slst in same st as beg.

2nd–5th points: 1slst in next sc, ch3, 1slst in 2nd ch from hook, 1sc in next ch, 1slst in same st as beg, ending with 1slst to join. (See Fig 8 on p. 14.)

Fasten off leaving a tail to sew with. Attach 4 stars to collar and one star to front of hat as shown in pictures. Weave in all ends.

Finishing: sew buttons securely to front of suit.

SAILOR HAT

Ch3 does not count as first dc.

Follow rnds 1–3 for all hat sizes

Rnd 1: With MC, ch3, 12dc in 3rd ch from hook. Skip ch3, slst to first dc. (12dc)

Rnd 2: Ch1, 2dc in same st as joining, 2dc in each dc around. Slst to top of dc to join rnd. (24dc)

Rnd 3: Ch1, *1dc in same st as joining, 2dc in next dc* rep from * to* around. Slst to top of dc to join rnd. (36dc)

0–3 months hat 13" x 5"

Rnd 4: Ch1, 1dc in same st as joining, 1dc in next dc, 2dc in next dc, *1dc in next 2dc, 2dc in next dc* rep from * to* around. Slst to top of dc to join rnd. (48dc)

Rnds 5–8: Ch1, 1dc in same st as joining, 1dc in each dc around. Slst to join rnd. (48dc)

Rnd 9: Ch1, 1dc in same st as joining, 1dc in next 2dc, dc tog next 2dc, 1dc in next 3dc, *dc tog next 2dc, 1dc in next 3dc* rep from * to * around. (39dc)

Rnd 10: Ch1, 1dc in same st as joining, 1dc in each dc around. Slst to join rnd. (39dc) Turn. Continue on to Cuff on Hat instructions.

3–6 months hat 14" x 5"

Rnd 4: Ch1, 1dc in same st as joining, 1dc in next dc, 2dc in next dc, *1dc in next 2dc, 2dc in next dc* rep from * to* around. Slst to top of dc to join rnd. (48dc)

Rnd 5: Ch1, 1dc in same st as joining, 1dc in next 10dc, 2dc in next dc, *1dc in next 11dc, 2dc in next dc* rep from * to* around. Slst to top of dc to join rnd. (52dc)

Rnds 6–8: Ch1, 1dc in same st as joining, 1dc in each dc around. Slst to join rnd. (52dc)

Rnd 9: Ch1, 1dc in same st as joining, 1dc in next 2dc, dc tog next 2dc, *1dc in next 3dc, dc tog next 2dc* rep from * to * around ending with 1dc in last 2dc. (42dc)

Rnd 10: Ch1, 1dc in same st as joining, 1dc in each dc around. Slst to join rnd. (42dc) Turn. Continue on to Cuff on Hat instructions.

6–12 months hat 15" x 5.5"
Rnd 4: Ch1, 1dc in same st as joining, 1dc in next dc, 2dc in next dc, *1dc in next 2dc, 2dc in next dc* rep from * to* around. Slst to top of dc to join rnd. (48dc)

Rnd 5: Ch1, 1dc in same st as joining, 1dc in next 2dc, 2dc in next dc, *1dc in next 3dc, 2dc in next dc* rep from * to * around. Slst to top of dc to join rnd. (60dc)

Rnds 6–9: Ch1, 1dc in same st as joining, 1dc in each dc around. Slst to join rnd. (60dc)

Rnd 10: Ch1, 1dc in same st as joining, 1dc in next 2dc, dc tog next 2dc, 1dc in next 3dc, *dc tog next 2dc, 1dc in next 3dc* rep from * to * around. (48dc)

Rnd 11: Ch1, 1dc in same st as joining, 1dc in each dc around. Slst to join rnd. (48dc) Turn. Continue on to Cuff on Hat instructions.

12–18 months hat 16" x 6"
Rnd 4: Ch1, 1dc in same st as joining, 1dc in next dc, 2dc in next dc, *1dc in next 2dc, 2dc in next dc* rep from * to* around. Slst to top of dc to join rnd. (48dc)

Rnd 5: Ch1, 1dc in same st as joining, 1dc in next 2dc, 2dc in next dc, *1dc in next 3dc, 2dc in next dc* rep from * to * around. Slst to top of dc to join rnd. (60dc)

Rnd 6: Ch1, 1dc in same st as joining, 1dc in next 13dc, 2dc in next dc, *1dc in next 14dc, 2dc in next dc* rep from * to * around. Slst to top of dc to join rnd. (64dc)

Rnds 7–10: Ch1, 1dc in same st as joining, 1dc in each dc around. Slst to join rnd. (64dc)

Rnd 11: Ch1, 1dc in same st as joining, 1dc in next 2dc, dc tog next 2dc, 1dc in next 3dc, *dc tog next 2dc, 1dc in next 3dc* rep from * to * around ending with 1dc in last dc. (52dc)

Rnd 12: Ch1, 1dc in same st as joining, 1dc in each dc around. Slst to join rnd. (52dc) Turn. Continue onto Cuff on Hat instructions.

18–24 months hat 16.5" x 6"
Rnd 4: Ch1, 1dc in same st as joining, 1dc in next dc, 2dc in next dc, *1dc in next 2dc, 2dc in next dc* rep from * to * around. Slst to top of dc to join rnd. (48dc)

Rnd 5: Ch1, 1dc in same st as joining, 1dc in next 2dc, 2dc in next dc, *1dc in next 3dc, 2dc in next dc* rep from * to * around. Slst to top of dc to join rnd. (60dc)

Rnd 6: Ch1, 1dc in same st as joining, 1dc in next 8dc, 2dc in next dc, *1dc in next 9dc, 2dc in next dc* rep from * to * around. Slst to top of dc to join rnd. (66dc)

Rnds 7–11: Ch1, 1dc in same st as joining, 1dc in each dc around. Slst to join rnd. (66dc)

Rnd 12: Ch1, 1dc in same st as joining, 1dc in next 2dc, dc tog next 2dc, 1dc in next 3dc, *dc tog next 2dc, 1dc in next 3dc* rep from * to * around, ending with 1dc in last dc. (53dc)

Rnd 13: Ch1, 1dc in same st as joining, 1dc in each dc around. Slst to join rnd. (53dc) Turn. Continue on to Cuff on Hat instructions.

Cuff on Hat for all sizes
Rnd 1: Add another strand of MC so that you are working double stranded for all the following rnds. Ch1, 1sc in BL of each dc around. Slst to join. (39sc, 42sc, 48sc, 52sc, 53sc)

Rnd 2: Ch1, 1sc in same st as joining, 1sc in each sc around. Slst to join. (39sc, 42sc, 48sc, 52sc, 53sc) Change to CC.

Rnds 3–4: With 2 strands of CC, ch1, 1sc in same st as joining, 1sc in each sc around. Slst to join. (39sc, 42sc, 48sc, 52sc, 53sc) Change to MC.

Rnds 5–6: With 2 strands of MC, ch1, 1sc in same st as joining, 1sc in each sc around. Slst to join. (39sc, 42sc, 48sc, 52sc, 53sc) Change to CC.

Rnds 7–8: With 2 strands of CC, ch1, 1sc in same st as joining, 1sc in each sc around. Slst to join. (39sc, 42sc, 48sc, 52sc, 53sc) Fasten off and weave in ends.

Crowns

Once upon a time there was a royal family with a royal infant. Too young to wear a crown of gold and jewels, the royal valet crocheted a majestic headpiece worthy of the royal infant. Whether playing dress-up or attending an inauguration, this crown is perfect for the little royal in your life. And they all lived happily ever after. The end.

Yarn

Cascade 220 Superwash 3.5oz/100gr/220yds/200m/ #4 medium weight

Colors used in pictures:

Color number 836 / Color name: Pink Ice x 1 skein

Color number 849 / Color name: Dark Aqua x 1 skein

Needle

US H8/5.00mm Susan Bates hook

Yarn Needle

Gauge

H hook = 12sc x 13sc rows = 4"

Glossary of Abbreviations

st(s) = stitch(es)

sk = skip

rnd(s) = round(s)

slst = slip stitch

ch = chain

sc = single crochet

dc = double crochet

rep from * to * = repeat between the stars

Rep from * to *= repeat what is between the stars

large shell = 1dc, 1trc, 1dtrc, 1trc, 1dc all in vst

vst = (1dc, ch1, 1dc) all in same st

fpsc = front post single crochet: insert hook under post of next sc, complete as a single crochet

cross stitch dc: sk next st, 1dc in next st, then go back and work 1dc in skipped st

Finished Sizes

0–3 months = 14" circumference

3–6 months = 15.5" circumference

6–12 months = 16.5" circumference

12–18 months = 17.5" circumference

18–24 months = 18.5" circumference

Instructions are written 0–3, other sizes are in parenthesis

CROWNS

With desired color and H hook, ch50 (ch60, ch70, ch80, ch90), join ch to first ch to form a circle.

Rnd 1: Ch1, 1sc in same ch as joining, 1sc in each ch around. Slst to join rnd. (50sc, 60sc, 70sc, 80sc, 90sc). (See Fig 1.)

Rnd 2: Ch1, 1fpsc around each sc around. Slst to join. (50fpsc, 60fpsc, 70fpsc, 80fpsc, 90fpsc). (See Fig 2.)

Rnd 3: Ch1, 1sc in the sts behind each fpsc around. Slst to join. (50sc, 60sc, 70sc, 80sc, 90sc). (See Fig 3.)

Rnd 4: Ch3, cross dc stitch around. 1dc in last st. Slst to join rnd. (50dc, 90dc, 70dc, 80dc, 90dc). (See Fig 4.)

Rnd 5: Ch1, 1sc in each dc around. Slst to join. (50dc, 60sc, 70sc, 80sc, 90sc)

Rnd 6: Ch4, 1dc in same st as joining, ch3, sk next 4sc, 1sc in next sc, ch3, sk next 4sc, *vst in next sc, ch3, sk next 4sc, 1sc in next sc, ch3, sk next 4sc* rep from * to * around. Slst to join. (See Figs 5 and 6.)

Rnd 7: Ch1, *large shell in vst, ch3, 1sc in next sc, ch3* rep from * to * around. Slst to join. (See Fig 7.)

Rnd 8: Ch1, slst, ch1 in next st, slst in next st, ch3, slst in same st, slst in next st, ch1, slst in next st, ch3, 1sc in next sc, ch3, *slst in next dc, ch1, slst in next trc, ch1, slst in next dtrc, ch3, slst in same st, slst in next trc, ch1, slst in next dc, ch3, 1sc in next sc, ch3* rep from * to * around. Slst to join. Fasten off and weave in ends. (See Fig 8.)

Crown stitches

(Fig 1) rnd 1 sc in each ch.

(Fig 2) front post single crochet (fpsc).

(Fig 3) sc behind the fpsc.

(Fig 4) cross stitch.

(Fig 5) 5 vst.

(Fig 6) 5 vst.

(Fig 7) large shell.

(Fig 8) last rnd.

Fisherman Vest

With a fresh twist on a fisherman's sweater, this unisex vest showcases a beautiful berry stitch that brings to mind the flavor of the classic Irish knits, but done in crochet. This exclusive design is tailored to allow for more movement giving your youngster the freedom to crawl or run in absolute comfort.

Yarn

Cascade 220 Superwash 3.5oz/100g/220yds/200m/
  #4 medium weight
Colors used in pictures:
Color number 809 / Color name: Really Red x 1 (1, 2, 2, 2) skeins
or Color number 862 / Color name: Walnut Heather x 1 (1, 2, 2, 2) skeins

Needle

US F5/3.75mm Susan Bates hook
US H8/5.00mm Susan Bates hook

Gauge

Note: you want your ribbing rows to measure approx 1" less than
  chest size.

0–3 months: ribbing rows 8" across – body approx 9" across
Chest circumference total approx = 18"
Vest Length – 5.5" to underarm, 3.5" to top of shoulder = 9" length
3–6 months: ribbing rows 8.5" across, body approx 9.5" across
Chest circumference total approx = 19"
Vest Length – 6.5" to underarm, 4" to top of shoulder = 10.5"
6–12 months: ribbing rows 9" across, body approx 10" across
Chest circumference total approx = 20"
Vest Length – 7" to underarm, 4.5" to top of shoulder = 11.5" length

12–18 months: ribbing rows 9.5" across, body approx 10.5" across
Chest circumference total approx = 21"
Vest Length – 8" to underarm, 4" to top of shoulder = 12" length
18–24 months: ribbing rows 10" across, body approx 11" across
Chest circumference total approx = 22"
Vest Length 9" to underarm, 4.25" to top of shoulder = 13.25" length

Glossary of Abbreviations

st(s) = stitch(es)
sc = single crochet
dc = double crochet
ch = chain(s)
yo = yarn over hook

slst = slip stitch
sctog2 = single crochet
  together next 2sc
fpdc = front post double
  crochet

BS = Berry Stitch: insert hook in next st, yo, pull through st
  (2loops on hook, keep first loop on hook): working with 2nd
loop only, ch3, yo, pull through 2 loops on hook; sc in next sc

fpdc = front post double crochet: Yo and draw up a loop
  around post, (yo and draw through 2 loops on hook) twice

Finished Sizes

0–3 months, 3–6 months, 6–12 months, 12–18 month,
  18–24 months
Instructions are written 0–3, other sizes are in parenthesis

VEST (See Figs 1 and 2)

Note: front and back of vest are worked the same. Make 2.

Ribbing Rows

Row 1: With F hook, ch6, 1sc in 2nd ch from hook, 1sc in the rem chs. Turn. (5sc)

Row 2: Ch1, 1sc in back loop of each sc across. Turn. (5sc)

Rows 3–29 (3–31, 3–33, 3–37, 3–39): Ch1, 1sc in the back loop of each sc across. Turn. (5sc). (See Fig 1 opposite for Row 3.)

End of ribbing rows, do not turn.

Body of Vest

Row 1: Change to H hook and turn ribbing on to its side. Ch1, working in the ends of rows, 1sc in each end of row. Turn. (29sc, 31sc, 33sc, 37sc, 39sc). (See Fig 2 opposite.)

Row 2: Ch1, 1sc in next 8sc (9sc, 10sc, 11sc, 12sc) 1dc in next 2sc, 1sc in next 4sc (4sc, 4sc, 5sc, 5sc), 1BS in next sc, 1sc in next 4sc, (4sc, 4sc, 5sc, 5sc), 1dc in next 2sc, 1sc in next 8sc (9sc, 10sc, 11sc, 12sc). Turn. (29sts, 31sts, 33sts, 37sts, 39sts)

Row 3: Ch1, 1sc in each st across. Turn. (29sc, 31sc, 33sc, 37sc, 39sc)

Row 4: Ch1, 1sc in next 8sc (9sc, 10sc, 11sc, 12sc), 1fpdc around next 2dc from previous row, 1sc in next 3sc (3sc, 3sc, 4sc, 4sc), 1BS in next sc, 1sc in next sc, 1BS in next sc, 1sc in next 3sc (3sc, 3sc, 4sc, 4sc), 1fpdc around next 2dc from previous row, 1sc in next 8sc (9sc, 10sc, 11sc, 12sc). Turn. (29sts, 31sts, 33sts, 37sts, 39sts)

Row 5: Ch1, 1sc in each st across. Turn. (29sc, 31sc, 33sc, 37sc, 39sc)

Row 6: Ch1, 1sc in next 8sc (9sc, 10sc, 11sc, 12sc), 1fpdc around next 2fpdc from previous row, 1sc in next 4sc (4sc, 4sc, 5sc, 5sc), 1BS in next sc, 1sc in next 4sc (4sc, 4sc, 5sc, 5sc), 1fpdc around next 2fpdc from previous row, 1sc in next 8sc (9sc, 10sc, 11sc, 12sc). Turn. (29sts, 31sts, 33sts, 37sts, 39sts)

Row 7: Ch1, 1sc in each st across. Turn. (29sc, 31sc, 33sc, 37sc, 39sc)

Row 8: Ch1, 1sc in next 8sc (9sc, 10sc, 11sc, 12sc), 1fpdc around next 2fpdc from previous row, 1sc in next 3sc (3sc, 3sc, 4sc, 4sc), 1BS in next sc, 1sc in next sc, 1BS in next sc, 1sc in next 3sc (3sc, 3sc, 4sc, 4sc), 1fpdc around next 2fpdc from previous row, 1sc in next 8sc (9sc, 10sc, 11sc, 12sc). Turn. (29sts, 31sts, 33sts, 37sts, 39sts)

Row 9: Ch1, 1sc in each st across. Turn. (29sc, 31sc, 33sc, 37sc, 39sc)

Rows 10–19, (10–23, 10–27, 10–31, 10–35): Repeat rows 6–9 in sequence, or desired length to underarm, ending with row 7.

Row 20 (24, 28, 32, 36): For armholes, slst in first 5sc, 1sc in next 3sc, (4sc, 5sc, 6sc, 7sc), 1fpdc around next 2fpdc from previous row, 1sc in next 3sc (3sc, 3sc, 4sc, 4sc), 1BS in next sc, 1sc in next sc, 1BS in next sc, 1sc in next 3sc (3sc, 3sc, 4sc, 4sc), 1fpdc around next 2fpdc from previous row, 1sc in next 3sc (4sc, 5sc, 6sc, 7sc). Leave last 5sc unworked. Turn. (19sts, 21sts, 23sts, 27sts, 29sts). (See Fig 3 opposite for Rows 20, 24, 28, 32, 26.)

Row 21 (25, 29, 33, 37): Ch1, 1sc in each st across. Turn. (19sc, 21sc, 23sc, 27sc, 29sc)

Row 22 (26, 30, 34, 38): Ch1, 1sc in next 3sc (4sc, 5sc, 6sc, 7sc), 1fpdc around next 2fpdc from previous row, 1sc in next 4sc (4sc, 4sc, 5sc, 5sc), 1BS in next sc, 1sc in next 4sc (4sc, 4sc, 5sc, 5sc), 1fpdc around next 2fpdc from previous row, 1sc in next 3sc (4sc, 5sc, 6sc, 7sc). Turn. (19sts, 21sts, 23sts, 27sts, 29sts)

Row 23 (27, 31, 35, 39): Ch1, 1sc in each st across. Turn. (19sc, 21sc, 23sc, 27sc, 29sc)

Row 24 (28, 32, 36, 40): Ch1, 1sc in next 3sc (4sc, 5sc, 6sc, 7sc), 1fpdc around next 2fpdc from previous row. 1sc in next 3sc (3sc, 3sc, 4sc, 4sc), 1BS in next sc, 1sc in next sc, 1BS in next sc, 1sc in next 3sc (3sc, 3sc, 4sc, 4sc), 1fpdc around next 2fpdc from previous row, 1sc in next 3sc (4sc, 5sc, 6sc, 7sc). Turn. (19sts, 21sts, 23sts, 2/sts, 29sts)

Row 25 (29, 33, 37, 41): Ch1, 1sc in each st across. Turn. (19sc, 21sc, 23sc, 27sc, 29sc)

Rows 26–33 (30–35, 34–41, 38–43, 42–49): Repeat rows 22–25, 26–29, 30–33, 34–37, 38–41 in sequence. Continue on to first shoulder shaping.

First Shoulder

Row 34 (36, 42, 44, 50): Ch1, 1sc in next 3sts (4sts, 5sts, 6sts, 7sts), 1fpdc around next 2fpdc from previous row. Turn, leaving rest of row unworked. (5sts, 6sts, 7sts, 8sts, 9sts). (See Fig 4 opposite for Rows 34, 36, 42, 44, 50.)

Row 35 (37, 43, 45, 51): Ch1, 1sc in each st across. Turn (5sc, 6sc, 7sc, 8sc, 9sc)

Row 36 (38, 44, 46, 52): Ch1, 1sc in next 3sc (4sc, 5sc, 6sc, 7sc) fpdc2tog. Turn. (4sts, 5sts, 6sts, 7sts, 8sts)

Row 37 (39, 45, 47, 53): Ch1, sc2tog, 1sc in next 2sc (3sc, 4sc, 5sc, 6sc). Turn. (3sts, 4sts, 5sts, 6sts, 7sts)

Row 38 (40, 46, 48, 54): Ch1, 1sc in next 3sts (4sts, 5sts, 6sts, 7sts). (3sts, 4sts, 5sts, 6sts, 7sts). (See Fig 5 below for Rows 38, 40, 46, 48, 54 showing whole first side finished.)
Fasten off leaving about 8" tail to sew with.

Second Shoulder

Row 34 (36, 42, 44, 50): With right side of vest facing you, count over to the left 9sts (9sts, 9sts, 11sts, 11sts), attach yarn in the 10th st (10th st, 10th st, 11th st, 11th st), ch1, 1fpdc around next 2fpdc from previous row, 1sc in next 3sc (4sc, 5sc, 6sc, 7sc). Turn (5sts, 6sts, 7sts, 8sts, 9sts). (See Fig 4 below for Rows 34, 36, 42, 44, 50.)

Row 35 (37, 43, 45, 51): Ch1, 1sc in each st across. Turn. (5sc, 6sc, 7sc, 8sc, 9sc)

Row 36 (38, 44, 46, 52): Ch1, fpdc2tog, 1sc in next 3sc (4sc, 5sc, 6sc, 7sc). Turn. (4sts, 5sts, 6sts, 7sts, 8sts)

Row 37 (39, 45, 47, 53): Ch1, 1sc in next 2sc (3sc, 4sc, 5sc, 6sc) sc2tog. (3sts, 4sts, 5sts, 6sts, 7sts)

Row 38 (40, 46, 48, 54): ch1, 1sc in next 3sts (4sts, 5sts, 6sts, 7sts). (3sts, 4sts, 5sts, 6sts, 7sts). Fasten off leaving about an 8" tail.

Next: with right sides facing each other, sew shoulder seams together. Sew sides of vest from ribbing rows to underarms. Weave in all ends. Turn vest right side out now.

Neck and Armhole Ribbing

Rnd1: With F hook, attach yarn to any st on neck or armhole edge, 1sc in each st around entire opening. Slst to join. (38sc, 38sc, 38sc, 44sc, 44sc). (See Fig 5 below). You now are going to be working in rows to make the ribbing.

Row 1: Ch4, 1sc in 2nd ch from hook, 1sc in next 2ch. Slst in same st as joining, 1sc in next 2sc from rnd1. Turn. (3sc)

Row 2: Ch1, Skip the 2sc and the slst, 1sc in the back loop of next 3sc. Turn. (3sc)

Row 3: Ch1, 1sc in the back loop of next 3sc, slst in same slst as before, 1sc in next 2sc on rnd1. (3sc)

Row 4: Ch1, skip the 2sc and the slst, 1sc in the back loop of next 3sc. Turn. (3sc)

Rest of ribbing rows
Repeat rows 3 and 4 alternately until you come to the other side of the opening, ending with row 4. Fasten off leaving a tail to sew with. Sew row 1 to last row to complete edge ribbing.

Fisherman Vest stitches

(Fig 1) working in the backloop of ribbing rows.

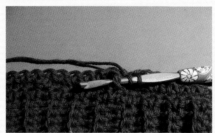
(Fig 2) working across ends of ribbing rows.

(Fig 3) forming armholes.

(Fig 4) forming shoulder stitches.

(Fig 5) shoulder to ribbing.

Fox Coverall

What does the fox say? Well, if it's your little angel in disguise, they would say how warm they are in this Cascade Superwash wool coverall. Your cub will be snug as a bug in a rug!

Yarn

Cascade 220 Superwash 3.5oz/100g/220yds/200m/
#4 medium weight

Colors used in pictures:

Color number 862 / Color name: Walnut Heather x 3 (4, 4, 5, 5) skeins

Color number 871 / Color name: White x 2oz

Color number 825 / Color name: Orange: small amount

6 x 1" buttons

Needle

US G6/4.00mm Susan Bates hook

US H8/5.00mm Susan Bates hook

Tapestry Needle

Gauge

2sc, 4fpdc, 4sc, 2fpdc, 2sc x 19sc rows = 4"

Glossary of Abbreviations

st(s) = stitch(es)

sk =skip

chsp = chain space

slst = slip stitch

rnd(s) = round(s)

tog = together

sp = space

yo = yarn over

rem = remaining

ch = chain

sc = single crochet

dc = double crochet

hdc = half double crochet

rep from * to * = repeat from between the stars

fpdc = front post double crochet: yo and draw up a loop around post, (yo and draw through 2 loops on hook) twice

fptrc = front post treble crochet: yo twice and draw up a loop around post, (yo and draw through 2 loops on hook) 3 times

To form the twist: yo twice and skip the next two fpdc, insert hook around third fpdc and yo and bring yarn back through, yo and drop off first two loops on hook, yo and drop off next 2 loops on hook, yo and drop of last 2 loops on hook – front post treble made, fptrc around the 4th fpdc, then go back to the skipped fpdc and fptrc around the 1st fpdc and then the 2nd fpdc

vshell = (2dc, ch1, 2dc) all in next sc or ch1s

Finished Sizes

0–3 months = approx 17" chest – shoulder to crotch approx 12"

3–6 months = approx 18" chest – shoulder to crotch approx 13"

6–12 months = approx 19" chest – shoulder to crotch approx 14"

12–18 months = approx 20" chest – shoulder to crotch approx 15"

18–24 months = approx 22" chest – shoulder to crotch approx 17"

Instructions are written 0–3, other sizes in parenthesis

BODICE
(Note: See Fox Coverall stitches p. 32)

All sizes: work to row 6.

Row 1: With G hook and desired MC, ch36 (ch39, ch42, ch45, ch48), 1sc in 2nd ch from hook, 1sc in each rem ch. Turn. 35sc (38sc, 41sc, 44sc, 47sc)

Row 2: Ch3, 1dc in next 4sc (5sc, 5sc, 6sc, 6sc), vshell, 1dc in next 5sc (5sc, 6sc, 6sc, 7sc), vshell, 1dc in next 11sc (12sc, 13sc, 14sc, 15sc), vshell, 1dc in next 5sc (5sc, 6sc, 6sc, 7sc), vshell, 1dc in next 5sc (6sc, 6sc, 7sc, 7sc). Turn. (47dc, 50dc, 53dc, 56dc, 59dc)

Row 3: Ch3, 1dc in next 6dc (7dc, 7dc, 8dc, 8dc), vshell, 1dc in next 9dc (9dc, 10dc, 10dc, 11dc), vshell, 1dc in next 15dc (16dc, 17dc, 18dc, 19dc), vshell, 1dc in next 9dc (9dc, 10dc, 10dc, 11dc), vshell, 1dc in next 7dc (8dc, 8dc, 9dc, 9dc). Turn. (63dc, 66dc, 69dc, 72dc, 75dc)

Row 4: Ch3, 1dc in next 8dc, (9dc, 9dc, 10dc, 10dc), vshell, 1dc in next 13dc (13dc, 14dc, 14dc, 15dc), vshell, 1dc in next 19dc (20dc, 21dc, 22dc, 23dc), vshell, 1dc in next 13dc (13dc, 14dc, 14dc, 15dc), vshell, 1dc in next 9dc (10dc, 10dc, 11dc, 11dc). Turn. (79dc, 82dc, 85dc, 88dc, 91dc)

Row 5: Ch3, 1dc in next 10dc (11dc, 11dc, 12dc, 12dc), vshell, 1dc in next 17dc, (17dc, 18dc, 18dc, 19dc), vshell, 1dc in next 23dc (24dc, 25dc, 26dc, 27dc), vshell, 1dc in next 17dc (17dc, 18dc, 18dc, 19dc), vshell, 1dc in next 11dc (12dc, 14dc, 13dc, 13dc). Turn. (95dc, 98dc, 101dc, 104dc, 107dc)

Row 6: Ch3, 1dc in next 12dc (13dc, 13dc, 14dc, 14dc), vshell, 1dc in next 21dc (21dc, 22dc, 22dc, 23dc), vshell, 1dc in next 27dc (28dc, 29dc, 30dc, 31dc), vshell, 1dc in next 21dc (21dc, 22dc, 22dc, 23dc), vshell, 1dc in next 13dc (14dc, 14dc, 15dc, 15dc). Turn. (111dc, 114dc, 117dc)

Continue on to form armhole openings for first 3 sizes, continue with bodices for last 2 sizes (120dc, 123dc)

Size 12–18 months only Bodice
Row 7: Ch3, 1dc in next 16dc vshell, 1dc in next 26dc, vshell, 1dc in next 34dc, vshell, 1dc in next 26dc, vshell, 1dc in next 17dc. Turn. (136dc) Continue on to form armhole openings.

Size 18–24 months only Bodice
Row 7: Ch3, 1dc in next 16dc, vshell, 1dc in next 27dc, vshell, 1dc in next 35dc, vshell, 1dc in next 27dc, vshell, 1dc in next 17dc. Turn. (139dc)

Row 8: Ch3, 1dc in next 18dc, vshell, 1dc in next 31dc, vshell, 1dc in next 39dc, vshell, 1dc in next 31dc, vshell, 1dc in next 19dc. Turn. (155dc) Continue on to form armhole openings.

Forming Armhole Openings
Row 1: Ch3, 1dc in next 14dc (15dc, 15dc, 18dc, 20dc), 1dc in next ch1sp, sk next 25dc (25dc, 26dc, 30dc, 35dc), 1dc in next ch1sp, 1dc in next 31dc (32dc, 33dc, 38dc, 43dc), 1dc in next ch1sp, sk next 25dc (25dc, 26dc, 30dc, 35dc), 1dc in next ch1sp, 1dc in next 15dc (16dc, 16dc, 19dc, 21dc). Turn. (65dc, 68dc, 69dc, 80dc, 89dc). (See Fig 1 on p. 32.)

PANTS
Change to H hook.

Row 1: With H hook, ch1, *1sc in next 4dc, 2sc in next dc* rep from * to* across. Turn. (78sc, 81sc, 82sc, 91sc, 108sc)

For size (0–3 months): Follow as written for row 1. (78sc)
For size (3–6 months): 1sc in last 3dc. (81sc)
For size (6–12 months): Follow as written for row 1. (82sc)
For size (12–18 months): 1sc in last dc. (91sc)
For size (18–24 months): 2sc in last dc. (108sc)

Row 2: Ch1, 1sc in next 3sc (4sc, 5sc, 3sc, 5sc), 1dc in next 2sc, *1sc in next 4sc (4sc, 4sc, 4sc, 5sc), 1dc in next 4sc, 1sc in next 4sc (4sc, 4sc, 4sc, 5sc), 1dc in next 2sc* rep from * to * across to last 3sc (5sc, 5sc, 2sc, 5sc), 1sc in last 3sc (5sc, 5sc, 2sc, 5sc). Turn. (78sts, 81sts, 82sts, 91sts, 108sts)

Row 3: Ch1, 1sc in each st across. Turn. (78sc, 80sc, 82sc, 91sc, 108sc)

Row 4: Ch1, 1sc in next 3sc (4sc, 5sc, 3sc, 5sc), 1fpdc around next 2dc from 2 previous rows, *1sc in next 4sc (4sc, 4sc, 4sc, 5sc), 1fpdc around next 4dc from 2 previous rows, 1sc in next 4sc (4sc, 4sc, 4sc, 5sc), 1fpdc around next 2dc from 2 previous rows* rep from * to * across to last 3sc (5sc, 5sc, 2sc, 5sc), 1sc in last 3sc (5sc, 5sc, 2sc, 5sc). Turn. (78sts, 81sts, 82sts, 91sc, 108sts)

Row 5: Ch1, 1sc in each st across. Turn. (78sc, 80sc, 82sc, 91sc, 108sc)

Row 6: Ch1, 1sc in next 3sc (4sc, 5sc, 3sc, 5sc), 1fpdc around next 2fpdc from 2 previous rows, *1sc in next 4sc (4sc, 4sc, 4sc, 5sc), 1fpdc around next 4fpdc from 2 previous rows, 1sc in next 4sc (4sc, 4sc, 4sc, 5sc), 1fpdc around next 2fpdc from 2 previous rows* rep from * to * across to last 3sc (5sc, 5sc, 2sc, 5sc), 1sc in last 3sc (5sc, 5sc, 2sc, 5sc). Turn. (78sts, 81sts, 82sts, 91sts, 108sts)

Row 7: Ch1, 1sc in each st across. Turn.
(78sc, 81sc, 82sts, 91sc, 108sc)

Note: the next row you will form the twist in the cable.

Row 8: Ch1, 1sc in next 3sc (4sc, 5sc, 3sc, 5sc), 1fpdc around next 2fpdc from 2 previous rows, *1sc in next 4sc (4sc, 4sc, 4sc, 5sc), (forming the twist) Twist over next 4 fpdc from 2 previous rows, (see pattern stitches), 1sc in next 4sc (4sc, 4sc, 4sc, 5sc), 1fpdc around next 2fpdc from 2 previous rows* rep from * to * across to last 3sc, (5sc, 5sc, 2sc, 5sc) 1sc in last 3sc (5sc, 5sc, 2sc, 5sc).Turn. (78sts, 81sts, 82sts, 91sts, 108sts). (See Figs 2–5 on p. 32.)

Row 9: Ch1, 1sc in each st across. Turn.
(78sc, 81sc, 82sts, 91sc, 108sc)

Row 10: Ch1, 1sc in next 3sc (4sc, 5sc, 3sc, 5sc), 1fpdc around next 2fpdc from 2 previous rows, *1sc in next 4sc (4sc, 4sc, 4sc, 5sc), 1fpdc around next 4fptrc from 2 previous rows, 1sc in next 4sc (4sc, 4sc, 4sc, 5sc), 1fpdc around next 2fpdc from2 previous rows* rep from * to * across to last 3sc (5sc, 5sc, 2sc, 5sc), 1sc in last 3sc (5sc, 5sc, 2sc, 5sc). Turn. (78sts, 81sts, 82sts, 91sts, 108sts)

Row 11: Ch1, 1sc in each st across. Turn.
(78sc, 81sc, 82sts, 91sc, 108sc)

Row 12: Ch1, 1sc in next 3sc (4sc, 5sc, 3sc, 5sc), 1fpdc around next 2dc from 2 previous rows, *1sc in next 4sc (4sc, 4sc, 4sc, 5sc), 1fpdc around next 4dc from 2 previous rows, 1sc in next 4sc (4sc, 4sc, 4sc, 5sc), 1fpdc around next 2dc from 2 previous rows* rep from * to * across to last 3sc (5sc, 5sc, 2sc, 5sc), 1sc in last 3sc (5sc, 5sc, 2sc, 5sc). Turn. (78sts, 81sts, 82sts, 91sts, 108sts)

Row 13: Ch1, 1sc in each st across. Turn.
(78sc, 81sc, 82sc, 91sc, 108sc)

Row 14: Ch1, 1sc in next 3sc (4sc, 5sc, 3sc, 5sc), 1fpdc around next 2fpdc from 2 previous rows, *1sc in next 4sc (4sc, 4sc, 4sc, 5sc), 1fpdc around next 4fpdc from 2 previous rows, 1sc in next 4sc (4sc, 4sc, 4sc, 5sc), 1fpdc around next 2fpdc from 2 previous rows* rep from * to * across to last 3sc (5sc, 5sc, 2sc, 5sc), 1sc in last 3sc (5sc, 5sc, 2sc, 5sc). Turn. (78sts, 81sts, 82sts, 91sts, 108sts)

Next: repeat rows 7–14 in sequence until shoulder to crotch measures approx

0–3 months shoulder to crotch approx 11"
3–6 months shoulder to crotch approx 12"
6–12 months shoulder to crotch approx 14"
12–18 monthsshoulder to crotch approx 15"
18–24 monthsshoulder to crotch approx 16"

BUTTONBANDS
For girls the button holes are on the right side.
For boys the button holes are on the left side.
To make a button hole just ch1 and sk next sc.

Row 1: Work in ends of rows up right front side, 1sc in each end of row. Turn.

Row 2: Ch1, sc in each sc across adding buttonholes evenly spaced across and making as many as desired. Turn. (If working button holes for a girl then do button holes on right side; if for a boy wait until you get to the left side to do the button holes).

Row 3: Ch1, 1sc in each sc and in each ch across.

Neck Edge
Row 1: 1sc in each st across neck edge over to left front side.

Left Front Band
Row 1: 1sc in ends of rows. Turn.

Rows 2–3: Ch1, 1sc in each sc across. Turn.

FIRST LEG
Rnd 1: Working on the wrong side, overlap button hole band over button band, working through both thicknesses, 1sc, then working on the leg, 1sc in next 38sts (40sc, 41sc, 45sc, 54sc) then working through both thicknesses, fold flat and pick up a loop from the front and a loop from the back and sc tog. Slst to join rnd. Turn. (38sc, 40sc, 41sc, 45sc, 54sc)

Next: Continue working in established pattern for leg until leg measures approx 5" (5.5", 6.5", 7", 8"). Slst to to join all rnds and turn.

Leg Cuffs
make 2
Rnd 1: Ch1, 1sc in same st as joining, 1sc in each st around and at the same time, decrease rnd 1 by 7sts. Slst to join rnd. Turn.

Rnds 2–16: Ch1, 1sc in same st as joining, 1sc in each sc around. Slst to join. Turn.

SECOND LEG

Rnd 1: Attach yarn to inside of leg. Sc in each st around 2nd leg. Slst to join. Turn.

Next: Continue working in established pattern for leg until leg measures approx 5" (5.5", 6.5", 7", 8"). Slst to to join all rnds and turn. Repeat cuff same as for first cuff. Fasten off and weave in all ends.

SLEEVES
make 2

Rnd 1: Attach yarn to any inside st in underarm, 1sc in each st around, making sure to increase to the final stitch counts that I have here. Slst to join rnd. Turn. (30sc, 30sc, 30sc, 36sc, 36sc)

Rnd 2: Ch1, 1sc in same st as joining, 1sc in next 8sc, (8sc, 8sc, 11sc, 11sc), 1dc in next 2sc, 1sc in next 2sc, 1dc in next 4sc, 1sc in next 2sc, 1dc in next 2sc, 1sc in next 9sc, (9sc, 9sc, 12sc, 12sc). Slst to join rnd. Turn. (30sts, 30sts, 30sts, 36sts, 36sts)

Rnd 3: Ch1, 1sc in same st as joining, 1sc in each st around. Slst to join rnd. Turn. (30sc, 30sc, 30sc, 36sc, 36sc)

Rnd 4: Ch1, 1sc in same st as joining, 1sc in next 8sc, (8sc, 8sc, 11sc, 11sc), 1fpdc around next 2dc from 2 previous rnds, 1sc in next 2sc, 1fpdc around next 4dc from 2 previous rnds, 1sc in next 2sc, 1fpdc around next 2dc from 2 previous rnds, 1sc in next 9sc, (9sc, 9sc, 12sc, 12sc), Slst to join rnd. Turn. (30sts, 30sts, 30sts, 36sts, 36sts)

Rnd 5: Ch1, 1sc in same st as joining, 1sc in each st around. Slst to join rnd. Turn. (30sc, 30sc, 30sc, 36sc, 36sc)

Rnd 6: Ch1, 1sc in same st as joining, 1sc in next 8sc, (8sc, 8sc, 11sc, 11sc), 1fpdc around next 2fpdc from 2 previous rnds, 1sc in next 2sc, 1fpdc around next 4fpdc from 2 previous rnds, 1sc in next 2sc, 1fpdc around next 2fpdc from 2 previous rnds, 1sc in next 9sc, (9sc, 9sc, 12sc, 12sc), Slst to join rnd. Turn. (30sts, 30sts, 30sts, 36sts, 36sts)

Rnd 7: Ch1, 1sc in same st as joining, 1sc in each st around. Slst to join rnd. Turn. (30sc, 30sc, 30sc, 36sc, 36sc)

Note: In this round you will form the twist in the cable.

Rnd 8: Ch1, 1sc in same st as joining, 1sc in next 8sc, (8sc, 8sc, 11sc, 11sc), 1fpdc around next 2fpdc from 2 previous rnds, 1sc in next 2sc, (forming the twist). Twist over next 4 fpdc, from 2 previous rnds, (see Pattern Stitches), *1sc in next 2sc, 1fpdc around next 2fpdc from 2 previous rnds, 1sc in next 9sc, (9sc, 9sc, 12sc, 12sc)* rep from * to * around. Slst to join rnd. Turn. (30sts, 30sts, 30sts, 36sts, 36sts)

Rnd 9: Ch1, 1sc in same st as joining, 1sc in each st around. Slst to join rnd. Turn. (30sc, 30sc, 30sc, 36sc, 36sc)

Rnd 10: Ch1, 1sc in same st as joining, 1sc in next 8sc, (8sc, 8sc, 11sc, 11sc), 1fpdc around next 2fpdc from 2 previous rnds, 1sc in next 2sc, 1fpdc around next 4fptrc from 2 previous rnds, 1sc in next 2sc, 1fpdc around next 2fpdc from 2 previous rnds, 1sc in next 9sc, (9sc, 9sc, 12sc, 12sc), Slst to join rnd. Turn. (30sts, 30sts, 30sts, 36sts, 36sts)

Rnd 11: Ch1, 1sc in same st as joining, 1sc in each st around. Slst to join rnd. Turn. (30sc, 32sc, 34sc, 36sc, 38sc)

Rnd 12: Ch1, 1sc in same st as joining, 1sc in next 8sc, (8sc, 8sc, 11sc, 11sc), 1fpdc around next 2fpdc from 2 previous rnds, 1sc in next 2sc, 1fpdc around next 4fpdc from 2 previous rnds, 1sc in next 2sc, 1fpdc around next 2fpdc from 2 previous rnds, 1sc in next 9sc, (9sc, 9sc, 12sc, 12sc), Slst to join rnd. Turn. (30sts, 30sts, 30sts, 36sts, 36sts)

Rnd 13: Ch1, 1sc in same st as joining, 1sc in each st around. Slst to join rnd. Turn. (30sc, 30sc, 30sc, 36sc, 36sc)

Rnd 14: Ch1, 1sc in same st as joining, 1sc in next 8sc, (8sc, 8sc, 11sc, 11sc) 1fpdc around next 2fpdc from 2 previous rnds, 1sc in next 2sc, 1fpdc around next 4fpdc from 2 previous rnds, 1sc in next 2sc, 1fpdc around next 2fpdc from 2 previous rnds, 1sc in next 9sc, (9sc, 9sc, 12sc, 12sc), Slst to join rnd. Turn. (30sts, 30sts, 30sts, 36sts, 36sts)

Rnd 15: Ch1, 1sc in same st as joining, 1sc in each st around. Slst to join rnd. Turn. (30sc, 30sc, 30sc, 36sc, 36sc)

Rnd 16: Ch1, 1sc in same st as joining, 1sc in next 8sc, (8sc, 8sc, 11sc, 11sc), 1fpdc around next 2fpdc from 2 previous rnds, 1sc in next 2sc, (forming the twist). Twist over next 4 fpdc, from 2 previous rnds, (see Pattern Stitches), *1sc in next 2sc, 1fpdc around next 2fpdc from 2 previous rnds, 1sc in next 9sc, (9sc, 9sc, 12sc, 12sc)* rep from * to * around. Slst to join rnd. Turn. (30sts, 30sts, 30sts, 36sts, 36sts)

Continue in established pattern until sleeve measures approx 5" (5.5", 6", 6.5", 7").

Fox Coverall stitches

(Fig 1) See row 1 armhole openings. (See p. 28.)

(Fig 2) 2nd fptrc. (See p. 29.)

(Fig 3) 3rd fptrc. (See p. 29.)

(Fig 4) 4th fptrc. (See p. 29.)

(Fig 5) formed twist cable. (See p. 29.)

Sleeve Cuff
make 2

Rnd 1: Ch1, 1sc in same st as joining, 1sc in next each st around. Slst to join rnd. Turn. (30sts, 30sts, 30sts, 36sts, 36sts)

Rnd 2: Ch1, 1sc in same st as joining, 1sc in next 2sc, sc2tog, *1sc in next 3sc, sc2tog* rep from * to * around. Slst to join. Turn. (24sts, 24sts, 24sts, 28sts, 28sts)

Rnds 3–16: Ch1, 1sc in same st as joining, 1sc in each sc around. Slst to join. Turn. (24sts, 24sts, 24sts, 28sts, 28sts)

HOOD

Row 1: with H hook, attach yarn to 4th st on inside of neck edge, skipping the first 3 sts, 1sc in next sc, *2sc in next sc, 1sc in next sc* rep from * to * across neck edge, to last 3sc, leaving last 3 ends of band rows unworked. Turn. (52sc, 59sc, 61sc, 66sc, 70sc)

Row 2: 1sc in next 4sc (7sc, 2sc, 4sc, 6sc), 1dc in next 2sc, *1sc in next 4sc, 1dc in next 4sc, 1sc in next 4sc, 1dc in next 2sc* rep from * to * across to last 4sc (6sc, 1sc, 4sc, 6sc), 1sc in last 4sc (6sc, 1sc, 4sc, 6sc). Turn. (52sts, 59sts, 61sts, 66sts, 70sts)

Row 3: 1sc in each st across. Turn. (52sc, 59sc, 61sc, 66sc, 70sc)

Row 4: 1sc in next 4sc (7sc, 2sc, 4sc, 6sc), 1fpdc around next 2dc from 2 previous rows, *1sc in next 4sc, 1fpdc around next 4dc from 2 previous rows, 1sc in next 4sc, 1fpdc around next 2dc from 2 previous rows* rep from * to * across to last 4sc (6sc, 1sc, 4sc, 6sc), 1sc in last 4sc (6sc, 1sc, 4sc, 6sc). Turn. (52sts, 59sts, 61sts, 66sts, 70sts)

Row 5: 1sc in each st across. Turn. (52sc, 59sc, 61sc, 66sc, 70sc)

Row 6: 1sc in next 4sc (7sc, 2sc, 4sc, 6sc), 1fpdc around next 2fpdc from 2 previous rows, *1sc in next 4sc, 1fpdc around next 4fpdc from 2 previous rows, 1sc in next 4sc, 1fpdc around next 2fpdc from 2 previous rows* rep from * to * across to last 4sc (6sc, 1sc, 4sc, 6sc), 1sc in last 4sc (6sc, 1sc, 4sc, 6sc). Turn. (52sts, 59sts, 61sts, 66sts, 70sts)

Row 7: 1sc in each st across. Turn. (52sc, 59sc, 61sc, 66sc, 70sc)

Row 8: 1sc in next 4sc (7sc, 2sc, 4sc, 6sc), 1fpdc around next 2fpdc from 2 previous rows, *1sc in next 4sc, (forming the twist). Twist over next 4 fpdc, from 2 previous rows, (see Pattern Stitches), 1sc in next 4sc, 1fpdc around next 2fpdc from 2 previous rows* rep from * to * across to last 4sc (6sc, 1sc, 4sc, 6sc), 1sc in last 4sc (6sc, 1sc, 4sc, 6sc). Turn. (52sts, 59sts, 61sts, 66sts, 70sts)

Row 9: 1sc in each st across. Turn. (52sc, 59sc, 61sc, 66sc, 70sc)

Row 10: 1sc in next 4sc (7sc, 2sc, 4sc, 6sc), 1fpdc around next 2fpdc from 2 previous rows, *1sc in next 4sc, 1fpdc around next 4fptrc from 2 previous rows, 1sc in next 4sc, 1fpdc around next 2fpdc from 2 previous rows* rep from * to * across to last 4sc (6sc, 1sc, 4sc, 6sc) 1sc in last 4sc (6sc, 1sc, 4sc, 6sc). Turn. (52sts, 59sts, 61sts, 66sts, 70sts)

Row 11: 1sc in each st across. Turn. (52sc, 59sc, 61sc, 66sc, 70sc)

Row 12: 1sc in next 4sc (7sc, 1sc, 4sc, 6sc), 1fpdc around next 2fpdc from 2 previous rows, *1sc in next 4sc, 1fpdc around next 4fpdc from 2 previous rows, 1sc in next 4sc, 1fpdc around next 2fpdc from 2 previous rows* rep from * to * across to last 4sc (6sc, 1sc, 4sc, 6sc) 1sc in last 4sc (6sc, 1sc, 4sc, 6sc). Turn. (52sts, 59sts, 61sts, 66sts, 70sts)

Row 13: 1sc in each st across. Turn. (52sc, 59sc, 61sc, 66sc, 70sc)

Row 14: 1sc in next 4sc (7sc, 2sc, 4sc, 6sc), 1fpdc around next 2fpdc from 2 previous rows, *1sc in next 4sc, 1fpdc around next 4fpdc from 2 previous rows, 1sc in next 4sc, 1fpdc around next 2fpdc from 2 previous rows* rep from * to * across to last 4sc (6sc, 1sc, 4sc, 6sc), 1sc in last 4sc (6sc, 1sc, 4sc, 6sc). Turn. (52sts, 59sts, 61sts, 66sts, 70sts)

Row 15: 1sc in each st across. Turn. (52sc, 59sc, 61sc, 66sc, 70sc)

Repeat rows 8–15 until hood measures approx 6.5" (7", 7.5", 8", 8.5")

Next: fold the last rnd in half. Working on wrong side, sc tog the two sides to form the hood. Fasten off and weave in ends.

Next: attach yarn to bottom of hood on the front ends of rows. Work sc all around front of hood in ends of rows. Fasten off and weave in ends.

EARS
make 2 (optional)
Ears
make 2 (Inside Orange)
Ears
make 2 (Outside Brown)
Note: make orange ears first.

Rnd 1: With G hook and Orange or Walnut Heather, ch10, 1sc in 2nd ch from hook, 1sc in next 2ch, 1hdc in next 3ch, 1dc in next 2ch, 5dc in last ch. Now working on opposite side of ch, 1dc in next 2ch, 1hdc in next 3ch, 1sc in last 3ch. Slst in sp between next 2sts. (21sts)

Rnd 2: Ch1, 1sc in same st as slst, 1sc in next 7sc, 2sc in next 5sc, 1sc in last 8sc. (26sc) Fasten off Orange and put aside for now.

Joining Orange to Walnut Heather ears.

Rnd 1: Hold orange ear in front of brown ear, and with Walnut Heather, working through both thicknesses, 1sc in each sc around. Fasten off leaving a tail to sew with. Sew ears to side of hood as shown in pictures.

TAIL
Rnd 1: With White, ch2, 4sc in 2nd ch from hook. (4sc).

Work in continuous rnds.

Rnd 2: (1sc in next sc, 2sc in next sc) x 2. (6sc)

Rnd 3: (1sc in next 2sc, 2sc in next sc) x 2. (8sc)

Rnd 4: (1sc in next 3sc, 2sc in next sc) x 2. (10sc)

Rnd 5: (1sc in next 4sc, 2sc in next sc) x 2. (12sc)

Rnds 6–8: 1sc in each sc around. (12sc)

Rnd 9: (1sc in next 4sc, sc2tog) x 2. (10sc) fasten off White.

Rnd 10: Attach Walnut Heather to any sc, ch1, 1hdc in same st as joining, 1hdc in each st around. (10hdc)

Work in continuous rnds.

Keep working around on the tail until about 10" long or to desired length, stuffing the tail lightly as you work. Fasten off leaving a tail. Sew tail onto coverall in the back, near the crotch so baby is not sitting on it.

Heirloom Afghan

A return to a time when everything was lacy and elegant, this light and airy heirloom afghan is the keepsake you're looking for. A delicate design in a cottage chic world, many generations will cherish this afghan for years to come.

Yarn
Cascade Cherub 1.75oz/50g/229m/210m/#2 baby weight
Color used in pictures:
Color number 01 / Color name: White x 6 skeins

Needle
US D3/3.25mm Susan Bates hook
Tapestry Needle

Gauge
18sc x 22sc rows = 4"

Pattern Notes
Weave in ends as work progresses.

Join with slip stitch as indicated unless otherwise stated.

Chain-3 at beginning of row/round counts as double crochet unless otherwise stated.

Glossary of Abbreviations
st(s) = stitch(es)
beg = beginning
sk = skip
rnd(s) = round(s)
slst = slip stitch
rep from * to * = repeat between the stars
BCS = Beginning Corner Shel: ch3, 2dc, ch1, 3dc all in same ch1sp
CS = Corner Shell: 3dc, ch1, 3dc all in same ch1sp
shell = 3dc in same sp
vst = (1dc, ch2, 1dc) all in same sp
Ch3 counts as first dc

chsp = chain space
ch = chain
sc = single crochet
dc = double crochet

Finished Size
Afghan measures approx 2ft x 3ft (61cm x 91cm)

AFGHAN

Row 1: Ch81, 1dc in 4th ch from hook, ch3, sk next 2ch, vst in next ch, ch3, sk next 2ch, *1sc in next 5ch, ch3, sk next 2ch, vst in next ch (see Pattern Stitches), ch3, sk next 2ch* rep from * to* across to last 2ch, 1dc in last 2ch. Turn. (See Fig 1 opposite)

Row 2: Ch3, 1dc in next dc, ch3, 7dc in vst, ch3, *sk next sc, 1sc in next 3sc, ch3, sk next sc, 7dc in vst, ch3* rep from * to * across to last 2dc, 1dc in last 2dc. Turn. (See Fig 2 opposite)

Row 3: Ch3, 1dc in next dc, ch3, (dc, ch1) in each of the next 6dc, dc in next dc, ch3, *sk next sc, 1sc in next sc, sk next sc, ch3, sk next ch3sp, (dc, ch1) in each of next 6dc, dc in next dc, ch3* rep from * to * across ending with 1dc in last 2dc. Turn. (See Fig 3 opposite)

Row 4: Ch3, 1dc in next dc, ch3, (sc, ch3) in each of next 6 ch1sps *sk next 2 ch3sps, (sc, ch3) in each of next 6 ch1sps* rep from * to * across ending last 1dc in last 2dc. Turn. (See Fig 4 opposite)

Row 5: Ch3, 1dc in next dc, ch3, sk next 3 ch3sps, vst in next ch3sp, ch3, sk next 2 ch3sps, *5sc in next ch3sp, ch3, sk next 2 ch3sps, vst in next ch3sp, ch3, sk next 2 ch3sps* rep from * to * across, 1dc in last 2dc. Turn.

Rows 6–41: rep rows 2–5 (to make 13 rows of large shells).

Rows 42–54: rep rows 2–4 once (to equal 14 rows of large shells) at the end of row 54, do not turn. (See Fig 5 opposite showing the details of Rows 42–54.)

Note: You now are going to work in rnds. Work it out so you have the same number of stitches on each long side and the same number of stitches on top and bottom

Rnd 1: Ch3, 2dc in beg st, 2dc in each end of rows on both long sides and on opposite side of ch work dc evenly across. And at the same time, when you get to the corner, work 3dc in each corner. When working on row 54, work (2dc in next ch3sp, 1dc in next ch3sp) rep from * around ending with 1dc in last dc. Slst to join rnd. (See Fig 6 opposite)

Rnd 2: Slst into next dc, BCS, *ch1, sk next 2dc, shell in next dc, rep from * to next ch1 corner sp. ** CS, rep from * around, ending with last rep at **, join to top of beg ch3.

Rnds 3–8: Slst into ch1sp, BCS, *(ch1, shell) in each ch1sp across to ch1 corner sp, ch1** CS, rep from * around, ending with last rep at **, join in top of beg ch3.

Rnd 9: Slst into ch1sp, BCS *1dc in each dc and chsp across to ch1 corner sp, ** CS, rep from *around ending with last rep at **, join to top of beg ch3.

Note: For rnd 10 you want to make sure that you start with a vst and end with a vst before and after each corner on the afghan. Adjust stitches if you need to make this work out.

Rnd 10: Slst to ch1sp, BCS, *ch3, sk next 2dc, vst in next dc, ch3, sk next 2dc, (1sc in next 5dc, ch3, sk next 2dc, vst in next dc, ch3) across to next ch1 corner sp** CS, rep from* around, ending last rep at **, join in top of beg ch3.

Rnd 11: Slst to ch1sp, BCS, *ch3, 7dc in vst, (ch3, sk next sc, 1sc in next 3sc, ch3, sk next sc, 7dc in next vst) across to ch3sp before corner, ch3** CS, rep from * around, ending with last rep at **, join in top of beg ch3.

Rnd 12: Slst to ch1sp, BCS, *ch3, sk next ch3sp, (dc, ch1) in each of the next 6dc, dc in next dc, (ch3, sk next sc, 1sc in next sc, sk next sc, ch3, sk next ch3sp, (dc, ch1) in each of next 6dc, dc in next dc) across to last ch3sp before corner, ch3, sk next ch3sp** CS, rep from * around, ending with last rep at **, join in top of beg ch3.

Rnd 13: Slst to ch1sp, BCS, *ch3, sk next ch3sp, (sc, ch3) in each of next 6 ch1sps (sk next 2 ch3sps, (sc, ch3) in each of next 6 ch1sps) across to next CS, sk next ch3sp** CS, rep from * around ending last rep at **, join in top of beg ch3.

Note: on rnd 14 you are going to be increasing a large shell on each end of each side of afghan. Starting with a vst in between CS and large shell and ending with a vst in between large shell and CS and you will be making the large shells alternate. They will not be lining up like they were when you first started this afghan.

Rnd 14: Slst over to ch1sp, BCS, *ch3, vst in next ch3sp, ch3, sk next 2 ch3sps, (5sc in next ch3sp, ch3, sk next 2 ch3sps, vst in next ch3sp, ch3) across to next CS** CS, rep from * around, ending last rep at **, join in top of beg ch3.

Rnd 15: Slst over to ch1sp, BCS, *ch3, sk next ch3sp, 7dc in vst, (ch3, sk next sc, 1sc in next 3sc, ch3, sk next sc, 7dc in vst) across to last ch3sp before corner, ch3, sk next ch3sp** CS, rep from * around, ending last rep at **, join in top of beg ch3.

Rnd 16: Slst over to ch1sp, BCS, (dc, ch1) in each of the next 6dc, dc in next dc, (ch3, sk next sc, 1sc in next sc, sk next sc, ch3, sk next ch3sp, (dc, ch1) in each of next 6dc, dc in next dc) across to last ch3sp before corner, ch3, sk next ch3sp** CS, rep from * around, ending last rep at **, join in top of beg ch3.

Rnds 17–20: Repeat rnds 13–16 once.

Rnd 21: repeat rnd 13.

Heirloom Afghan stitches

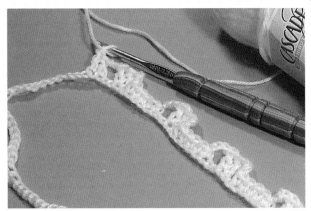

(Fig 1) row 1.

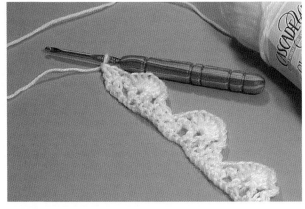

(Fig 2) row 2.

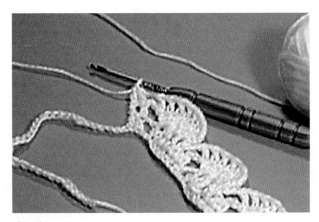

(Fig 3) row 3.

(Fig 4) row 4.

(Fig 5) middle stitches.

(Fig 6) corner stitches.

Lamb Afghan

Snuggled under this afghan made from comfy sheep's wool, your little lamb with be counting sheep in no time. And when nap time is over, this beautiful afghan also functions as a decorative wall hanging. Enjoy the scenery day or night. Who doesn't love a room with a view!

Yarn

Cascade 220 Superwash 3.5oz/100g/220yds/200m/ #4 medium weight

Colors used in pictures:

Color number 897 / Color name: Blue x 2 skeins

Color number 887 / Color name: Lime x 2 skeins

Color number 1917 / Color name: Brown x 2 skeins

Color number 890 / Color name: White x 2 skeins

Color number / Color name: Charcoal x 1 skein

Needle

US H8/5.00mm Susan Bates hook

Yarn Needle

Gauge

Gauge: 13vsc rows x 6.5vsc = 4"

Glossary of Abbreviations

st(s) = stitch(es)

yo = yarn over

rep = repeat

rem = remaining

sk = skip

tog = together

chsp = chain space

ch = chain

sc = single crochet

dc = double crochet

rep from * to * = repeat between the stars

vsc = v single crochet = (1sc, ch2, 1sc) all in the same stitch

vst = v stitch = (1dc, ch1, 1dc) all in same st

hbdc = herringbone double crochet – yo, insert hook into next st, yo and pull through the st and the first loop on the hook, yo and draw through one loop, yo and draw through both loops on hook

esc = extended single crochet – to make esc Insert hook in next st or row, yo, pull up loop, yo, pull through 1 loop on hook, yo, pull through 2 loops on hook

Finished Size

Afghan measures approx 2ft x 3ft (61cm x 91cm)

BLUE SKY
(Note: See Lamb Afghan stitches p. 43)

Row 1: With Blue, ch101, 1sc in 2nd ch from hook, sk next 2ch, *(1sc, ch2, 1sc) all in next ch, sk next 2ch* rep from * to * across to last 3ch, 1sc in last ch. Turn. (32 vsc)

Row 2: Ch1, 1sc in next sc, vsc in next ch2sp and in each ch2sp across, 1sc in last sc. Turn. (32vsc)

Repeat row 2 for 12 inches long. Fasten off and weave in ends.

GREEN GRASS
Row 1: Attach Green to first st, 1sc in same st as joining, 2esc in each hole below vsc from previous row across to last sc, 1sc in last sc. Turn. (See Figs 1 and 2 on p. 43.)

Rows 2–3: Ch1, 1sc in each st across. Turn. (66sc)

Note: On the rows that you will be changing colors, carry yarn across the row, working over the color you are not using and making color change in last step of stitch. You do not have to carry yarn across on rows 5–6 and 9–12. These rows you can just work with the Brown. Work rows 4–10 all in sc, changing colors as indicated on each row. (See Fig 3 on p. 43.)

Row 4: Ch1, *9green, 2brown* rep from * to * 4 more times, 11green. Turn. (66sc)

Rows 5–6: Change to Brown, ch1, 1sc in each st across. Turn. (66sc)

Row 7: Ch1, 11green, *2brown, 9green* rep from * to * 4 more times. Turn. (66sc)

Row 8: Ch1, *9green, 2brown* rep from * to * 4 more times, 11green. Turn. (66sc)

Rows 9–10: With Brown, ch1, 1sc in each st across. Turn. (66sc)

Row 11: Ch1, 11green, *2brown, 9green* rep from * to * 4 more times. Turn. (66sc) Fasten off Brown.

Row 12: With Green, ch1, 1hbdc in each st across. Turn. (66hbdc)

Repeat row 12 until Green measures approx 16inches long.

CURTAIN PANELS (MAKE 2)
Row 1: With G hook and White, ch30, 1sc in 2nd ch from hook, 1sc in each rem ch. Turn. (29sc)

Row 2: Ch1, 1dc in next 2sc, ch3, sk next 2sc, vst in next sc, ch3, sk next 2sc, *1sc in next 5sc, ch3, sk next 2sc, vst in next sc, ch3, sk next 2sc* rep from * to * one more time, 1dc in last 2sc. Turn.

Row 3: Ch1, 1dc in next 2dc, ch3, 7dc in vst, ch3, *sk next sc, 1sc in next 3sc, sk next sc, ch3, 7dc in vst, ch3* rep from * to * one more time, 1dc in last 2dc. Turn.

Row 4: Ch1, 1dc in next 2dc, ch3, 1dc in next dc (ch1, 1dc in next dc) x 6, ch3, *sk next sc, 1sc in next sc, sk next sc, ch3, 1dc in next dc (ch1, 1dc in next dc) x 6, ch3* rep from * to * one more time, 1dc in last 2dc. Turn.

Row 5: Ch1, 1dc in next 2dc, ch3, *1sc in next ch1sp, ch3* rep from * to * across working only in the ch1sps to last 2dc, 1dc in last 2dc. Turn.

Row 6: Ch1, 1dc in next 2dc, ch3, sk next 3 ch3sps, vst in next ch3sp, ch3, *sk next 2 ch3sps, 5sc in next ch3sp, ch3, sk next 2 ch3sps, vst in next ch3sp, ch3* rep from * to * one more time, sk next 3 ch3sps, 1dc in last 2dc. Turn.

Row 7: Ch1, 1dc in next 2dc, ch3, 7dc in vst, ch3, *sk next sc, 1sc in next 3sc, sk next sc, ch3, 7dc in vst, ch3* rep from * to * one more time, 1dc in last 2dc. Turn.

Row 8: Ch1, 1dc in next 2dc, ch3, 1dc in next dc (ch1, 1dc in next dc) x 6, ch3, *sk next sc, 1sc in next sc, sk next sc, ch3, 1dc in next dc (ch1, 1dc in next dc) x 6, ch3* rep from * to * one more time, 1dc in last 2dc. Turn.

Row 9: Ch1, 1dc in next 2dc, ch3, *1sc in next ch1sp, ch3* rep from * to * across working only in the ch1sps to last dc, 1dc in last 2dc. Turn.

Next repeat rows 6–9 in sequence 12 more times. For left curtain panel do not turn at end of last repeat.

LEFT CURTAIN PANEL
Row 1: Ch1, 1sc in each end of row, working it out so that you have 89sc. Turn. (89sc)

Row 2: Ch1, 1dc in next 2sc, ch3, sk next 2sc, vst in next sc, ch3, sk next 2sc, *1sc in next 5sc, ch3, sk next 2sc, vst in next sc, ch3, sk next 2sc* rep from * to * across to last 2sc, 1dc in last 2sc. Turn.

Row 3: Ch1, 1dc in next 2dc, ch3, 7dc in vst, ch3, *sk next sc, 1sc in next 3sc, sk next sc, ch3, 7dc in vst, ch3* rep from * to * across to last 2sts, 1dc in last 2dc. Turn.

Row 4: Ch1, 1dc in next 2dc, ch3, 1dc in next dc (ch1, dc in next dc) x 6, ch3, *sk next sc, 1sc in next sc, sk next sc, ch3, 1dc in next dc (ch1, dc in next dc) x 6, ch3* rep from * to * across to last 2sts, 1dc in last 2dc. Turn.

Row 5: Ch1, 1dc in next 2dc, ch3, *1sc in next ch1sp, ch3* rep from * to * across working only in the ch1sps to last dc, 1dc in last 2dc.

Next: find middle of afghan on top of sky, hold left panel to left side of afghan. Sc together, through both thicknesses, the top of the curtain panel to the top of the afghan. (33sc)

Then sc together through both thicknesses the long side of the curtain panel to the long side of the afghan. The counts can vary depending on the length of your afghan, so make sure to count how many sc you make for the left side and make sure to make the same number of sc for the right long side. Fasten off and make right curtain panel.

RIGHT CURTAIN PANEL

Row 1: Ch1, 1sc in each end of row on long side, 1sc in each st on opposite side of starting ch, 1sc in each end of row down 2nd long side, working it out so that you have 89sc on each long side. Turn.

Note: Rows 2–5: work only on one long side.

Row 2: Ch1, 1dc in next 2sc, ch3, sk next 2sc, vst in next sc, ch3, sk next 2sc, *1sc in next 5sc, ch3, sk next 2sc, vst in next sc, ch3, sk next 2sc* rep from * to * across to last 2sc, 1dc in last 2sc. Turn.

Row 3: Ch1, 1dc in next 2dc, ch3, 7dc in vst, ch3, *sk next sc, 1sc in next 3sc, sk next sc, ch3, 7dc in vst, ch3* rep from * to * across to last 2sts, 1dc in last 2dc. Turn.

Row 4: Ch1, 1dc in next 2dc, ch3, 1dc in next dc (ch1, dc in next dc) x 6, ch3, *sk next sc, 1sc in next sc, sk next sc, ch3, 1dc in next dc (ch1, dc in next dc) x 6, ch3* rep from * to * across to last 2sts, 1dc in last 2dc. Turn.

Row 5: Ch1, 1dc in next 2dc, ch3, *1sc in next ch1sp, ch3* rep from * to * across working only in the ch1sps to last dc, 1dc in last 2dc. Fasten off and weave in ends.

Hold right panel in front of afghan, sc long side together and top together to afghan. Fasten off and weave in ends.

Curtain Tie Backs – make 2
Row 1: With White, ch51, 1sc in 2nd ch from hook, 1sc in each rem ch. Turn. (50sc)

Row 2: 1sc in first sc, sk next sc, 5dc in next sc, sk next sc *1sc in next sc, sk next sc, 5dc in next sc, sk next sc* rep from * to * across. Fasten off leaving a tail to sew with. Using yarn needle, sew tie back to afghan as shown in picture.

WINDOW FRAME
Rnd 1: With Brown and G hook, attach yarn to any stitch on outside of afghan, 1hbdc in each st around entire afghan and at the same time, work 1hbdc, ch2, 1hbdc in each corner. Slst to join. Turn.

Rnds 2–5: Ch1, 1hbdc in each hbdc around, working 1hbdc, ch2, 1hbdc in each ch2sp around. Slst to join. Turn.

At the end of rnd 5 fasten off and weave in ends.

LAMBS
make as many as desired (See Figs 4–6 opposite)
Face: With Charcoal and G hook, ch4, 5dc in 4th ch from hook. Fasten off leaving a tail to sew with.

Body: Row 1: With White and G hook, attach to flat side of face, 1sc in next 5 ends of rows on face. Turn. (5sc)

Row 2: Ch1, sc in each sc across. Turn. (5sc)

Row 3: Ch1, 2sc in first sc, 1sc in next 3sc, 2sc in next sc. Turn. (7sc)

Row 4: Ch1, 2sc in first sc, 1sc in next 5sc, 2sc in next sc. Turn. (9sc)

Rows 5–8: Ch1, 1sc in each sc across. Turn. (9sc)

Row 9: sc2tog, 1sc in next 5sc, sc2tog. Turn. (7sc)

Row 10: sc2tog, 1sc in next 3sc, sc2tog. Turn. (5sc)

Row 11: sc2tog, 1sc in next sc, sc2tog. Turn. (3sc)

Row 12: Ch1, slst in next 3sc, slst across the next 10 ends of rows. Turn.

You now are going to work a rnd.

Rnd 1: Ch1, 1slst in same st as joining, *sk next st, 5sc in next st, sk next st, slst in next st* rep from * to * 2 more times, ch4, 1slst in 2nd ch from hook, 1slst in next 2ch, 1slst in same st as ch4, **sk next st, 5sc in next st, sk next st, 1slst in next st ** rep from ** to ** around. Slst to join. Fasten off leaving a long tail to sew sheep onto pasture in desired places.

Lamb Afghan stitches

(Fig 1) row 1 of grass. (See p. 40.)

(Fig 2) vsc. (See p. 40.)

(Fig 3) fence. (See p. 40.)

(Fig 4) lamb face. See oppisite to make the lambs.

(Fig 5) row one lamb body.

(Fig 6) lamb applique.

Lamb Coverall

True to a lamb's nature, this fisherman cable coverall is made with 100% wool fiber. But unlike most wool, this is an easy to care for yarn that is machine washable. Don't let the cold weather slow you down! Wrap your little loved ones in this snuggly warm coverall today.

Yarn

Cascade 220 Superwash 3.5oz/100g/220yds/200m/
  #4 medium weight

Colors used in pictures:

Color number 871 / Color name: White x 5 (5, 6, 6, 7) skeins

Color number 1941 / Color name: Hunter Green: small amount

Buttons

6 x 1" buttons

Needle

US G6/4.00mm Susan Bates hook

US H8/5.00mm Susan Bates hook

Tapestry Needle

Gauge

Gauge: G hook = 7sc + 6dc x 19sc rows = 4"

Glossary of Abbreviations

st(s) = stitch(es)	rem = remaining
yo = yarn over	rnd(s) = round(s)
sk =skip	sc = single crochet
sp = space	dc = double crochet

ch = chain	tog = together
slst = slip stitch	hdc = half double crochet
rep from * to * = repeat between the stars	trc = treble crochet

fpdc = front post double crochet: yo and draw up a loop around post, (yo and draw through 2 loops on hook) twice.

fptrc = front post treble crochet: yo twice and draw up a loop around post, (yo and draw through 2 loops on hook) 3 times.

To form the twist: yarn over twice and skip the next two fpdc, insert hook around third fpdc and yarn over and bring yarn back through, yarn over and drop off first two loops on hook, yarn over and drop of next 2 loops on hook, yarn over and drop of last 2 loops on hook. Front post treble made, fptrc around the 4th fpdc, then go back to the skipped fpdc and fptrc around the 1st fpdc and then the 2nd fpdc.

vshell = (2dc, ch1, 2dc) all in next sc or ch1sp.

Finished Sizes

0–3 approx 17" chest – shoulder to crotch approx 12"

3–6 approx 18" chest – shoulder to crotch approx 13"

6–12 approx 19" chest – shoulder to crotch approx 14"

12–18 approx 20" chest – shoulder to crotch approx 15"

18–24 approx 22" chest – shoulder to crotch approx 17"

Instructions are written 0–3, other sizes in parenthesis

BODICE

Work all sizes to row 6.

Row 1: With G hook and desired MC, ch36 (ch39, ch42, ch45, ch48), 1sc in 2nd ch from hook, 1sc in each rem ch. Turn. (35sc, 38sc, 41sc, 44sc, 47sc)

Row 2: Ch3, 1dc in next 4sc (5sc, 5sc, 6sc, 6sc), vshell, 1dc in next 5sc (5sc, 6sc, 6sc, 7sc,), vshell, 1dc in next 11sc (12sc, 13sc, 14sc, 15sc), vshell, 1dc in next 5sc (5sc, 6sc, 6sc, 7sc), vshell, 1dc in next 5sc (6sc, 6sc, 7sc, 7sc). Turn. (47dc, 50dc, 53dc, 56dc, 59dc)

Row 3: Ch3, 1dc in next 6dc (7dc, 7dc, 8dc, 8dc), vshell, 1dc in next 9dc (9dc, 10dc, 10dc, 11dc), vshell, 1dc in next 15dc (16dc, 17dc, 18dc, 19dc), vshell, 1dc in next 9dc (9dc, 10dc, 10dc, 11dc), vshell, 1dc in next 7dc (8dc, 8dc, 9dc, 9dc). Turn. (63dc, 66dc, 69dc, 72dc, 75dc)

Row 4: Ch3, 1dc in next 8dc, (9dc, 9dc, 10dc, 10dc), vshell, 1dc in next 13dc (13dc, 14dc, 14dc, 15dc), vshell, 1dc in next 19dc (20dc, 21dc, 22dc, 23dc), vshell, 1dc in next 13dc (13dc, 14dc, 14dc, 15dc), vshell, 1dc in next 9dc (10dc, 10dc, 11dc, 11dc). Turn. (79dc, 82dc, 85dc, 88dc, 91dc)

Row 5: Ch3, 1dc in next 10dc (11dc, 11dc, 12dc, 12dc), vshell, 1dc in next 17dc, (17dc, 18dc, 18dc, 19dc), vshell, 1dc in next 23dc (24dc, 25dc, 26dc, 27dc), vshell, 1dc in next 17dc (17dc, 18dc, 18dc, 19dc), vshell, 1dc in next 11dc (12dc, 12dc, 13dc, 13dc). Turn. (95dc, 98dc, 101dc, 104dc, 107dc)

Row 6: Ch3, 1dc in next 12dc (13dc, 13dc, 14dc, 14dc), vshell, 1dc in next 21dc (21dc, 22dc, 22dc, 23dc), vshell, 1dc in next 27dc (28dc, 29dc, 30dc, 31dc), vshell, 1dc in next 21dc (21dc, 22dc, 22dc, 23dc), vshell, 1dc in next 13dc (14dc, 14dc, 15dc, 15dc). Turn. (111dc, 114dc, 117dc),

Continue on to forming armhole openings for first 3 sizes, continue on to finish bodices for last 2 sizes (120dc, 123dc).

Size 12–18 months only Bodice

Row 7: Ch3, 1dc in next 16dc, vshell, 1dc in next 26dc, vshell, 1dc in next 34dc, vshell, 1dc in next 26dc, vshell, 1dc in next 17dc. Turn. (136dc) continue on to forming armhole openings.

Size 18–24 months only Bodice

Row 7: Ch3, 1dc in next 16dc, vshell, 1dc in next 27dc, vshell, 1dc in next 35dc, vshell, 1dc in next 27dc, vshell, 1dc in next 17dc. Turn. (139dc)

Row 8: Ch3, 1dc in next 18dc, vshell, 1dc in next 31dc, vshell, 1dc in next 39dc, vshell, 1dc in next 31dc, vshell, 1dc in next 19dc. Turn. (155dc) continue on to forming armhole openings.

Forming Armhole Openings

Row 1: Ch3, 1dc in next 14dc (15dc, 15dc, 18dc, 20dc), 1dc in next ch1sp, sk next 25dc (25dc, 26dc, 30dc, 35dc), 1dc in next ch1sp, 1dc in next 31dc (32dc, 33dc, 38dc, 43dc), 1dc in next ch1sp, sk next 25dc (25dc, 26dc, 30dc, 35dc), 1dc in next ch1sp, 1dc in next 15dc (16dc, 16dc, 19dc, 21dc). Turn. (65dc, 68dc, 69dc, 80dc, 89dc)

PANTS

Change to H hook.

Row 1: With H hook, ch1, *1sc in next 4dc, 2sc in next dc* rep from * to * across. Turn. (78sc, 81sc, 82sc, 91sc, 108sc)

See chart below to complete row 1 for different sizes:
For size 0–3 months: Follow as written for row 1. (78sc)
For size 3–6 months: 1sc in last 3dc. (81sc)
For size 6–12 months: Follow as written for *Row 1:* (82sc)
For size 12–18 months: 1sc in last dc (91sc)
For size 18–24 months: 1sc in last dc (108sc)

Row 2: Ch1, 1sc in next 3sc (4sc, 5sc, 3sc, 5sc), 1dc in next 2sc, *1sc in next 4sc (4sc, 4sc, 4sc, 5sc), 1dc in next 4sc, 1sc in next 4sc (4sc, 4sc, 4sc, 5sc), 1dc in next 2sc* rep from * to * across to last 3sc (5sc, 5sc, 2sc, 5sc), 1sc in last 3sc (5sc, 5sc, 2sc, 5sc). Turn. (78sts, 81sts, 82sts, 91sts, 108sts)

Row 3: Ch1, 1sc in each st across. Turn. (78sc, 81sc, 82sc, 91sc, 108sc)

Row 4: Ch1, 1sc in next 3sc (4sc, 5sc, 3sc, 5sc), 1fpdc around next 2dc from 2 previous rows, *1sc in next 4sc (4sc, 4sc, 4sc, 5sc), 1fpdc around next 4dc from 2 previous rows, 1sc in next 4sc (4sc, 4sc, 4sc, 5sc), 1fpdc around next 2dc from 2 previous rows* rep from * to * across to last 3sc (5sc, 5sc, 2sc, 5sc), 1sc in last 3sc (5sc, 5sc, 2sc, 5sc). Turn. (78sts, 81sts, 82sts, 91sts, 108sts)

Row 5: Ch1, 1sc in each st across. Turn. (78sc, 81sc, 82sc, 91sc, 108sc)

Row 6: Ch1, 1sc in next 3sc (4sc, 5sc, 3sc, 5sc), 1fpdc around next 2fpdc from 2 previous rows, *1sc in next 4sc (4sc, 4sc, 4sc, 5sc), 1fpdc around next 4fpdc from 2 previous rows, 1sc in next 4sc (4sc, 4sc, 4sc, 5sc), 1fpdc around next 2fpdc from 2 previous rows* rep from * to * across to last 3sc (5sc, 5sc, 2sc, 5sc), 1sc in last 3sc (5sc, 5sc, 2sc, 5sc). Turn. (78sts, 81sts, 82sts, 91sts, 108sts)

Row 7: Ch1, 1sc in each st across. Turn (78sc, 81sc, 82sc, 91sc, 108sc)

Note: this round you will form the twist in the cable.

Row 8: Ch1, 1sc in next 3sc (4sc, 5sc, 3sc, 5sc), 1fpdc around next 2fpdc from 2 previous rows, *1sc in next 4sc (4sc, 4sc, 4sc, 5sc), (forming the twist). Twist over next 4 fpdc from 2 previous rows, (see pattern stitches), 1sc in next 4sc (4sc, 4sc, 4sc, 5sc), 1fpdc around next 2fpdc from 2 previous rows* rep from * to * across to last 3sc, (5sc, 5sc, 2sc, 5sc) 1sc in last 3sc (5sc, 5sc, 2sc, 5sc). Turn. (78sts, 81sts, 82sts, 91sts, 108sts). (See Fig 1 below showing what the fptrc looks like.)

Row 9: Ch1, 1sc in each st across. Turn. (78sc, 81sc, 82sc, 91sc, 108sc)

Row 10: Ch1, 1sc in next 3sc (4sc, 5sc, 3sc, 5sc), 1fpdc around next 2fpdc from 2 previous rows, *1sc in next 4sc (4sc, 4sc, 4sc, 5sc), 1fpdc around next 4fptrc from 2 previous rows, 1sc in next 4sc

(4sc, 4sc, 4sc, 5sc), 1fpdc around next 2fpdc from 2 previous rows* rep from * to * across to last 3sc (5sc, 5sc, 2sc, 5sc), 1sc in last 3sc (5sc, 5sc, 2sc, 5sc). Turn. (78sts, 81sts, 82sts, 91sts, 108sts)

Row 11: Ch1, 1sc in each st across. Turn. (78sc, 81sc, 82sc, 91sc, 108sc)

Row 12: Ch1, 1sc in next 3sc (4sc, 5sc, 3sc, 5sc), 1fpdc around next 2dc from 2 previous rows, *1sc in next 4sc (4sc, 4sc, 4sc, 5sc), 1fpdc around next 4dc from 2 previous rows, 1sc in next 4sc (4sc, 4sc, 4sc, 5sc), 1fpdc around next 2dc from 2 previous rows* rep from * to * across to last 3sc (5sc, 5sc, 2sc, 5sc), 1sc in last 3sc (5sc, 5sc, 2sc, 5sc). Turn (78sts, 81sts, 82sts, 91sts, 108sts)

Row 13: Ch1, 1sc in each st across. Turn. (78sc, 81sc, 82sc, 91sc, 108sc)

Row 14: Ch1, 1sc in next 3sc (4sc, 5sc, 3sc, 5sc), 1fpdc around next

Lamb Coverall stitches

(Fig 1) fptrc form twist. (See Row 8 above.)

(Fig 2) working across neck edge. (See p. 49.)

(Fig 3) working in ends of rows. (See Buttonband p. 49.)

(Fig 4) overlap buttonbands. (See First Leg p. 49.)

(Fig 5) 1st leg opening. (See p. 49.)

2fpdc from2 previous rows, *1sc in next 4sc (4sc, 4sc, 4sc, 5sc), 1fpdc around next 4fpdc from 2 previous rows, 1sc in next 4sc (4sc, 4sc, 4sc, 5sc), 1fpdc around next 2fpdc from 2 previous rows* rep from * to * across to last 3sc (5sc, 5sc, 2sc, 5sc), 1sc in last 3sc (5sc, 5sc, 2sc, 5sc). Turn. (78sts, 81sts, 82sts, 91sts, 108sts)

Next: repeat rows 7–14 in sequence until shoulder to crotch measures approx

0–3 shoulder to crotch approx 11"
3–6 shoulder to crotch approx 12"
6–12 shoulder to crotch approx 14"
12–18 shoulder to crotch approx 15"
18–24 shoulder to crotch approx 16"

BUTTONBANDS

For girls the button holes are on the right side.
For boys the button holes are on the left side.
To make a button hole just ch1 and sk next sc.

Row 1: Working in ends of rows up right front side, 1sc in each end of row. Turn.

Row 2: Ch1, sc in each sc across adding buttonholes evenly spaced across and making as many as desired. Turn. (If working button holes for a girl then do button holes on right side; if for a boy wait until you get to the left side to do the button holes.) Turn.

Row 3: Ch1, 1sc in each sc and in each ch across.

Neck Edge

Row 1: 1sc in each st across neck edge over to left front side. (See Fig 2 on p. 47.)

Left Front Buttonband

Row 1: 1sc in ends of rows. Turn. (See Fig 3 on p. 47.)

Rows 2–3: Ch1, 1sc in each sc across. Turn.

FIRST LEG

Rnd 1: working on the wrong side, overlap button hole band over button band, working through both thicknesses, 1sc, then working on the leg, 1sc in next 38sts (40sts, 41sts, 45sts, 54sc), then working through both thicknesses, fold flat and pick up a loop from the front and a loop from the back and sc tog. Slst to join rnd. Turn. (38sc, 40sc, 41sc, 45sc, 54sc). (See Figs 4 and 5 on p. 47.)

Next: Continue working in established pattern for leg until leg measures approx 5" (5.5", 6.5", 7", 8"). Slst to to join all rnds and turn.

Leg Cuffs
make 2

Rnd 1: Ch1, 1sc in same st as joining, 1sc in each st around and at the same time, decrease rnd 1 by 7sts. Slst to join rnd. Turn.

Rnds 2–16: Ch1, 1sc in same st as joining, 1sc in each sc around. Slst to join. Turn.

Second Leg

Rnd 1: Attach yarn to inside of leg. Sc in each st around 2nd leg. Slst to join. Turn.

Next: Continue working in established pattern for leg until leg measures approx 5"(5.5", 6.5", 7", 8") Slst to to join all rnds and turn. Repeat cuff same as for first cuff. Fasten off and weave in all ends.

SLEEVES
make 2

Rnd 1: Attach yarn to any inside st in underarm, 1sc in each st around, increasing to the final stitch counts that I have here. Slst to join rnd. Turn. (30sc, 30sc, 30sc, 36sc, 36sc)

Rnd 2: Ch1, 1sc in same st as joining, 1sc in next 8sc, (8sc, 8sc, 11sc, 11sc), 1dc in next 2sc, 1sc in next 2sc, 1dc in next 4sc, 1sc in next 2sc, 1dc in next 2sc, 1sc in next 9sc, (9sc, 9sc, 12sc, 12sc). Slst to join rnd. Turn. (30sts, 30sts, 30sts, 36sts, 36sts)

Rnd 3: Ch1, 1sc in same st as joining, 1sc in each st around. Slst to join rnd. Turn. (30sc, 30sc, 30sc, 36sc, 36sc)

Rnd 4: Ch1, 1sc in same st as joining, 1sc in next 8sc, (8sc, 8sc, 11sc, 11sc) 1fpdc around next 2dc from 2 previous rnds, 1sc in next 2sc, 1fpdc around next 4dc from 2 previous rnds, 1sc in next 2sc, 1fpdc around next 2dc from 2 previous rnds, 1sc in next 9sc (9sc, 9sc, 12sc, 12sc) Slst to join rnd. Turn. (30sts, 30sts, 30sts, 36sts, 36sts)

Rnd 5: Ch1, 1sc in same st as joining, 1sc in each st around. Slst to join rnd. Turn. (30sc, 30sc, 30sc, 36sc, 36sc)

Rnd 6: Ch1, 1sc in same st as joining, 1sc in next 8sc (8sc, 8sc, 11sc, 11sc) 1fpdc around next 2fpdc from 2 previous rnds, 1sc in next 2sc, 1fpdc around next 4fpdc from 2 previous rnds, 1sc in next 2sc, 1fpdc around next 2fpdc from 2 previous rnds, 1sc in next 9sc (9sc, 9sc, 12sc, 12sc). Slst to join rnd. Turn. (30sts, 30sts, 30sts, 36sts, 36sts)

Rnd 7: Ch1, 1sc in same st as joining, 1sc in each st around. Slst to join rnd. Turn. (30sc, 30sc, 30sc, 36sc, 36sc)

Note: this round you will form the twist in the cable.

Rnd 8: Ch1, 1sc in same st as joining, 1sc in next 8sc (8sc, 8sc, 11sc, 11sc) 1fpdc around next 2fpdc from 2 previous rnds, 1sc in next 2sc, (forming the twist). Twist over next 4 fpdc, from 2 previous rnds, (see pattern stitches), *1sc in next 2sc, 1fpdc around next 2fpdc from 2 previous rnds, 1sc in next 9sc (9sc, 9sc, 12sc, 12sc). Slst to join rnd. Turn. (30sts, 30sts, 30sts, 36sts, 36sts)

Rnd 9: Ch1, 1sc in same st as joining, 1sc in each st around. Slst to join rnd. Turn. (30sc, 30sc, 30sc, 36sc, 36sc)

Rnd 10: Ch1, 1sc in same st as joining, 1sc in next 8sc (8sc, 8sc, 11sc, 11sc) 1fpdc around next 2fpdc from 2 previous rnds, 1sc in next 2sc, 1fpdc around next 4fptrc from 2 previous rnds, 1sc in next 2sc, 1fpdc around next 2fpdc from 2 previous rnds, 1sc in next 9sc (9sc, 9sc, 12sc, 12sc). Slst to join rnd. Turn. (30sts, 30sts, 30sts, 36sts, 36sts)

Rnd 11: Ch1, 1sc in same st as joining, 1sc in each st around. Slst to join rnd. Turn. (30sc, 30sc, 30sc, 36sc, 36sc)

Rnd 12: Ch1, 1sc in same st as joining, 1sc in next 8sc (8sc, 8sc, 11sc, 11sc), 1fpdc around next 2fpdc from 2 previous rnds, 1sc in next 2sc, 1fpdc around next 4fpdc from 2 previous rnds, 1sc in next 2sc, 1fpdc around next 2fpdc from 2 previous rnds, 1sc in next 9sc (9sc, 9sc, 12sc, 12sc). Slst to join rnd. Turn. (30sts, 30sts, 30sts, 36sts, 36sts)

Rnd 13: Ch1, 1sc in same st as joining, 1sc in each st around. Slst to join rnd. Turn. (30sc, 30sc, 30sc, 36sc, 36sc)

Rnd 14: Ch1, 1sc in same st as joining, 1sc in next 8sc (8sc, 8sc, 11sc, 11sc), 1fpdc around next 2fpdc from 2 previous rnds, 1sc in next 2sc, 1fpdc around next 4fpdc from 2 previous rnds, 1sc in next 2sc, 1fpdc around next 2fpdc from 2 previous rnds, 1sc in next 9sc (9sc, 9sc, 12sc, 12sc). Slst to join rnd. Turn. (30sts, 30sts, 30sts, 36sts, 36sts)

Rnd 15: Ch1, 1sc in same st as joining, 1sc in each st around. Slst to join rnd. Turn. (30sc, 30sc, 30sc, 36sc, 36sc)

Rnd 16: Ch1, 1sc in same st as joining, 1sc in next 8sc (8sc, 8sc, 11sc, 11sc), 1fpdc around next 2fpdc from 2 previous rnds, 1sc in next 2sc, (forming the twist). Twist over next 4 fpdc, from 2 previous rnds, (see pattern stitches), *1sc in next 2sc, 1fpdc around next

2fpdc from 2 previous rnds, 1sc in next 9sc (9sc, 9sc, 12sc, 12sc). Slst to join rnd. Turn. (30sts, 30sts, 30sts, 36sts, 36sts)

Continue in established pattern until sleeve measures approx 5" (5.5", 6", 6.5", 7")

Sleeve Cuff
make 2
Rnd 1: Ch1, 1sc in same st as joining, 1sc in each st around. Slst to join rnd. Turn. (30sts, 30sts, 30sts, 36sts, 36sts)

Rnd 2: Ch1, 1sc in same st as joining, 1sc in next 2sc, sc2tog, *1sc in next 3sc, sc2tog* rep from * to * around. Slst to join. Turn. (24sts, 24sts, 24sts, 28sts, 28sts)

Rnds 3–16: Ch1, 1sc in same st as joining, 1sc in each sc around. Slst to join. Turn. (24sts, 24sts, 24sts, 28sts, 28sts)

HOOD
Row 1: with H hook, attach yarn to 4th st on inside of neck edge, skipping the first 3 sts, 1sc in next sc, *2sc in next sc, 1sc in next sc, *across neck edge, to last 3sc, leaving last 3 ends of band rows unworked. Turn. (52sc, 59sc, 61sc, 66sc, 70sc)

Row 2: 1sc in next 4sc, (7sc, 2sc, 4sc, 6sc) 1dc in next 2sc, *1sc in next 4sc, 1dc in next 4sc, 1sc in next 4sc, 1dc in next 2sc* rep from * to * across to last 4sc (6sc, 1sc, 4sc, 6sc) 1sc in last 4sc (6sc, 1sc, 4sc, 6sc). Turn. (52sts, 59sts, 61sts, 66sts, 70sts)

Row 3: 1sc in each st across. Turn. (52sc, 59sc, 61sc, 66sc, 70sc)

Row 4: 1sc in next 4sc (7sc, 2sc, 4sc, 6sc), 1fpdc around next 2dc from 2 previous rows, *1sc in next 4sc, 1fpdc around next 4dc from 2 previous rows, 1sc in next 4sc, 1fpdc around next 2dc from 2 previous rows* rep from * to * across to last 4sc (6sc, 1sc, 4sc, 6sc), 1sc in last 4sc (6sc, 1sc, 4sc, 6sc). Turn. (52sts, 59sts, 61sts, 66sts, 70sts)

Row 5: 1sc in each st across. Turn. (52sc, 59sc, 61sc, 66sc, 70sc)

Row 6: 1sc in next 4sc (7sc, 2sc, 4sc, 6sc), 1fpdc around next 2fpdc from 2 previous rows, *1sc in next 4sc, 1fpdc around next 4fpdc from 2 previous rows, 1sc in next 4sc, 1fpdc around next 2fpdc from 2 previous rows* rep from * to * across to last 4sc (6sc, 1sc, 4sc, 6sc) 1sc in last 4sc (6sc, 1sc, 4sc, 6sc). Turn. (52sts, 59sts, 61sts, 66sts, 70sts)

Row 7: 1sc in each st across. Turn. (52sc, 59sc, 61sc, 66sc, 70sc)

Row 8: 1sc in next 4sc (7sc, 2sc, 4sc, 6sc), 1fpdc around next 2fpdc from 2 previous rows, *1sc in next 4sc, (forming the twist). Twist over next 4 fpdc, from 2 previous rows, (see pattern stitches), 1sc in next 4sc, 1fpdc around next 2fpdc from 2 previous rows* rep from * to * across to last 4sc (6sc, 1sc, 4sc, 6sc) 1sc in last 4sc (6sc, 1sc, 4sc, 6sc). Turn. (52sts, 59sts, 61sts, 66sts, 70sts)

Row 9: 1sc in each st across. Turn. (52sc, 59sc, 61sc, 66sc, 70sc)

Row 10: 1sc in next 4sc (7sc, 2sc, 4sc, 6sc), 1fpdc around next 2fpdc from 2 previous rows, *1sc in next 4sc, 1fpdc around next 4fptrc from 2 previous rows, 1sc in next 4sc, 1fpdc around next 2fpdc from 2 previous rows* rep from * to * across to last 4sc (6sc, 1sc, 4sc, 6sc), 1sc in last 4sc (6sc, 1sc, 4sc, 6sc). Turn. (52sts, 59sts, 61sts, 66sts, 70sts)

Row 11: 1sc in each st across. Turn. (52sc, 59sc, 61sc, 66sc, 70sc)

Row 12: 1sc in next 4sc (7sc, 1sc, 4sc, 6sc), 1fpdc around next 2fpdc from 2 previous rows, *1sc in next 4sc, 1fpdc around next 4fpdc from 2 previous rows, 1sc in next 4sc, 1fpdc around next 2fpdc from 2 previous rows* rep from * to * across to last 4sc (6sc, 1sc, 7sc, 6sc), 1sc in last 4sc (6sc, 1sc, 7sc, 6sc). Turn. (52sts, 59sts, 61sts, 66sts, 70sts)

Row 13: 1sc in each st across. Turn. (52sc, 59sc, 61sc, 66sc, 70sc)

Row 14: 1sc in next 4sc (7sc, 2sc, 4sc, 6sc) 1fpdc around next 2fpdc from 2 previous rows, *1sc in next 4sc, 1fpdc around next 4fpdc from 2 previous rows, 1sc in next 4sc, 1fpdc around next 2fpdc from 2 previous rows* rep from * to * across to last 4sc (6sc, 1sc, 4sc, 6sc), 1sc in last 4sc (6sc, 1sc, 4sc, 6sc). Turn. (52sts, 59sts, 61sts, 66sts, 70sts)

Row 15: 1sc in each st across. Turn. (52sc, 59sc, 61sc, 66sc, 70sc)

Repeat rows 8–15 until hood measures approx 6.5" (7", 7.5", 8", 8.5")

Next: fold the last rnd in half. Working on wrong side, sc tog the two sides to form the hood. Fasten off and weave in ends.

Next: attach yarn to bottom of hood on the front ends of rows. Work sc all around front of hood in ends of rows. Fasten off and weave in ends.

OPTIONAL EARS
make 2
Inside Hunter Green – make 2
Outside White Ears – make 2
Note: make 2 Hunter Green ears first.

Rnd 1: With H hook and Green or White, ch10, 1sc in 2nd ch from hook, 1sc in next 2ch, 1hdc in next 3ch, 1dc in next 2ch, 5dc in last ch. Now working on opposite side of ch, 1dc in next 2ch, 1hdc in next 3ch, 1sc in last 3ch. Slst in sp between next 2sts. (21sts)

Rnd 2: Ch1, 1sc in same st as slst, 1sc in next 7sc, 2sc in next 5sc, 1sc in last 8sc. (26sc) Fasten off Green and put aside for now.

Joining green to white ears.

Rnd 1: Hold green in front of white ear, and with White, working through both thicknesses, 1sc in each sc around. Fasten off leaving a tail to sew with. Sew ears to side of hood as shown in the pictures on pp. 44, 45, and 48.

Lacy Cardigan

Ideal for every day or that special occasion, this lacy sweater is a lovely addition to any wardrobe. Made with washable wool yarns from Cascade.

Yarn

Cascade 220 Superwash 3.5oz/100g/220yds/200m/ #4 medweight

Colors used in pictures:

Color number 836 / Color name: Pink Ice x 1 (2, 2, 3, 3) skeins

Color number 871 / Color name: White x 2oz

Color number 851 / Color name: Lime x 2oz

Buttons

3 x ½" buttons

Needle

US G6/4.00mm Susan Bates hook

Yarn Needle

Gauge

15dc x 9dc rows = 4"

Chest measurements

0–3 approx 17" chest

3–6 approx 18" chest

6–12 approx 19" chest

12–18 approx 20" chest

18–24 approx 22" chest

Glossary of Abbreviations

beg = beginning

slst = slip stitch

ch = chain

rnd(s) = round(s)

chsp = chain space

sc = single crochet

vst = 1dc, ch1, 1dc all in the same st

rep from * to * = repeat between the stars

dc = double crochet

BL – Back loop

rem = remaining

sp = space

sk = skip

Notes

Ch3 counts as first dc

Ch2 does not count as first dc

Ch1 does not count as first st

Finished Sizes

0–3 months, 3–6 months, 6–12 months, 12–18 months, 18–24 months

Instructions are written 0–3, other sizes are in parenthesis

BODICE
(Note: See Lacy Cardigan stitches p. 56)

Work rows 1–6 for all sizes. (See Fig 1 on p. 56 for yoke.)

Row 1: With G hook and Pink Ice, ch33 (35, 37, 39, 41), 1sc in 2nd ch from hook, 1sc in each rem ch. Turn. (32sc, 34sc, 36sc, 38sc, 40sc)

Row 2: Ch3, 2dc in next sc, *1dc in next sc, 2dc in next sc* rep from * to * across. Turn. (48dc, 51dc, 54dc, 57dc, 60dc)

Row 3: Ch3, 1dc in next dc, 2dc in next dc *1dc in next 2dc, 2dc in next dc* rep from * to * across. Turn. (64dc, 68dc, 72dc, 76dc, 80dc)

Row 4: Ch3, 1dc in next 2dc, 2dc in next dc, *1dc in next 3dc, 2dc in next dc* rep from * to * across. Turn. (80dc, 85dc, 90dc, 95dc, 100dc)

Row 5: Ch3, 1dc in next 3dc, 2dc in next dc, *1dc in next 4dc, 2dc in next dc* rep from * to * across. Turn. (96dc, 102dc, 108dc, 114dc, 120dc)

Row 6: Ch3, 1dc in next 4dc, 2dc in next dc, *1dc in next 5dc, 2dc in next dc* rep from * to * across. Turn. (112dc, 119dc, 126dc, 133dc, 140dc)

For sizes 0–3 months, 3–6 months, 6–12 months, stop after row 6 and continue on to form armhold openings.

12–18 months and 18–24 months ONLY
Row 7: Ch3, 1dc in next 5dc, 2dc in next dc, *1dc in next 6dc, 2dc in next dc* rep from * to * across. Turn. (152dc, 160dc)

Row 8: Ch3, 1dc in next 6dc, 2dc in next dc, *1dc in next 7dc, 2dc in next dc* rep from * to * across. Turn. (171dc, 180dc)

Continue on to form armhole openings.

Form Armhole Openings
Row 1: Ch3, 1dc in next 15dc (15dc, 16dc, 26dc, 30dc), sk next 24dc (26dc, 28dc, 30dc, 30dc) 1dc in next 32dc (35dc, 36dc, 57dc, 60dc) sk next 24dc (26dc, 28dc, 30dc, 30dc), 1dc in next 16dc (16dc, 17dc, 27dc, 30dc). Turn. (64dc, 67dc, 70dc, 111dc, 120dc). (See Fig 2 on p. 56.)

BODY
Row 1: Ch1, 1sc in same st as turning, ch5, *sk next 2dc, 1sc in next dc, ch5* rep from * to * across:

0–3 months: to last 3dc, sk next 2dc, 1sc in last dc. (21 ch3loops)
3–6 months: to last 6dc, sk next 5dc, 1sc in last dc. (21 ch3loops)
6–12 months: to last 3dc, sk next 2dc, 1sc in last dc. (23 ch3loops)
12–18 months: to last 2dc, sk next dc, 1sc in last dc. (37 ch3loops)
18–24 months: to last 5dc, sk next 4dc, 1sc in last dc. (38 ch3loops)

Row 2: Ch3, 3dc in next ch5sp, ch2, sc in next ch5sp, ch2, *(3dc, ch2) x2 in next ch5sp, sc in next ch5sp, ch2* rep from * to * across to last ch5sp, 3dc in last ch5sp, dc in last st. Turn. (See Fig 3 on p. 56.)

Row 3: Ch1, 1sc in same st as turning, ch3, 1dc in next 3dc, sk next 2 ch2sps, 1dc in next 3dc, ch3, *1sc in next ch2sp, ch3, 1dc in next 3dc, sk next 2 ch2sps, 1dc in next 3dc, ch3* rep from * to * across to last dc, sc in last dc. Turn.

Row 4: Ch1, 1dc in sc, ch3, sk next ch3sp, 1sc in next dc, ch5, sk next 4dc, 1sc in next dc, *ch5, sk next 2 ch3sps, 1sc in next dc, ch5, sk next 4dc, 1sc in next dc* rep from * to * across to last ch3sp, ch2, sk last ch3sp, dc in last sc. Turn.

Row 5: Ch1, 1sc in first dc, ch2, sk next ch2sp, (3dc, ch2) x2 in next ch5sp, *1sc in next ch5sp, ch2, (3dc, ch2) x2 in next ch5sp* rep from * to * across to last ch2sp, sk last ch2sp, 1sc in last dc. Turn.

Row 6: Ch3, sk next ch2sp, 1dc in next 3dc, ch3, 1sc in next ch2sp, ch3, 1dc in next 3dc, *sk next 2 ch2sps, 1dc in next 3dc, ch3, 1sc in next ch2sp, ch3, 1dc in next 3dc* rep from * to * across to last ch2sp, sk last ch2sp, dc in last sc. Turn.

Row 7: Ch1, 1dc in dc, ch2, sk first 2dc, 1sc in next dc, ch5, sk next 2 ch3sps, 1sc in next dc *ch5, sk next 4dc, 1sc in next dc, ch5, sk next 2 ch3sps, 1sc in next dc* rep from * to * across to last 3dc, ch2, sk next 2dc, 1dc in last dc. Turn.

Rows 8–19 (8–19, 8–19, 8–22, 8–22): Repeat rows 2–7 in sequence.

Row 20 (20, 20, 23, 23): Ch1, 1sc in beg st, 3sc in next ch2loop, 1sc in next sc, *4sc in next ch5loop, 1sc in next sc* rep from * to * across, ending with 3sc in last loop, 1sc in last st. Do not fasten off but continue on to buttonbands.

BUTTONBANDS
Right Buttonhole Band
Row 1: Ch1, 1sc in each end of row working 30sc (30sc, 30sc, 34sc, 34sc). Turn. (30sc, 30sc, 30sc, 34sc, 34sc)

Row 2: Ch1, 1sc in next sc, ch2, sk next sc, *1sc in next 5sc, ch2, sk next sc* rep from * to * 3 (3, 3, 4, 4) more times, 1sc in next 4 (4, 4, 2, 2sc). Turn.

Lacy Cardigan stitches

(Fig 1) yoke. (See p. 54.)

(Fig 2) forming armholes. (See Row 1 on p. 54.)

(Fig 3) row 2 of body. (See p. 54.)

(Fig 4) row 1 collar. (See p. 57.)

(Fig 5) BL on collar. (See p. 57.)

(Fig 6) row 3 collar. (See p. 57.)

(Fig 7) row 4 collar. See p. 57.

(Fig 8) row 5 collar. See p. 57.)

(Fig 9) row 6 collar. (See p. 57.)

Row 3: Ch1, 1sc in each sc and 1sc in each ch2sp across. (30sc, 30sc, 30sc, 34sc, 34sc) Do not fasten off but continue on to neck edge.

Neck Edge
Row 1: 1sc in each st across neck edge. (Count not important) do not fasten off but continue on to left button band.

Left Buttonband
Row 1: 1sc in each end of row working 30 (30, 30, 34, 34sc). Turn. (30sc, 30sc, 30sc, 34sc, 34sc)

Rows 2–3: 1sc in each sc across. Turn. (30sc, 30sc, 30sc, 34sc, 34sc)

At end of row 3 fasten off and weave in ends.

SLEEVES
make 2
All sizes

Rnd 1: With G and Pink Ice attach yarn to bottom of arm opening, Ch3, work 27dc, (29dc, 31dc, 33dc, 34dc) around arm opening. Slst to join rnd. Turn. (28dc, 30dc, 32dc, 34dc, 35dc)

Rnds 2–10 (2–10, 2–12, 2–14, 2–14): Ch1, 1dc in same st as joining, 1dc in each dc around. Slst to join rnds. Turn. (28dc, 30dc, 32dc, 34dc, 35dc)

Rnd 11 (11, 13, 15, 25): Ch1, 1dc in same st as joining, 1dc in each dc around. Slst to join rnds. (28dc, 30dc, 32dc, 34dc, 35dc) Fasten off and weave in ends.

Sleeve length:
0–3 months = approx 5"
3–6 months = 5"
6–12 months = 6.5"
12–18 months = 7.5"
18–24 months = 7.5"

Arm Cuff
Rnd 1: Attach White where you fastened off, ch1, 2sc in same st as joining, 2sc in each sc around. Slst to join rnd. (54dc, 60dc, 64dc, 68dc, 70dc)

Rnd 2: Ch1, 1dc in same st as joining, ch3, sk next 2sc *vst in next sc, ch3, sk next 2sc, 1sc in next 5sc, ch3, sk next 2sc* rep from * to * around. Slst to join rnd. (*Note:* if needed, adjust skipped sts so you end with the 5sc.)

Rnd 3: Ch1, 1dc in same st as joining, ch3, 7dc in vst, ch3, sk next sc, 1sc in next 3sc, ch3, sk next sc *7dc in vst, ch3, sk next sc, 1sc in next 3sc, ch3, sk next sc* rep from * to * around. Slst to join.

Rnd 4: Ch1, 1dc in same st as joining, ch3, 1dc (ch1, 1dc) x 6, ch3, *sk next sc, 1sc in next sc, sk next sc, ch3, 1dc (ch1, 1dc) x6, ch3*. Slst to join rnd. Fasten off and weave in ends.

Rnd 5: Attach Lime to where you fastened off, ch1, 1sc in same st as joining, (ch3, 1sc in next ch1sp,) rep around working only in the ch1sps. Slst to join. Fasten off and weave in ends.

COLLAR
Row 1: On outside of sweater, attach White to first sc on neck edge, 1sc in each sc across neck edge. Turn. (See photo opposite.)

Row 2: Ch1, 1sc in BL of each sc across neck edge. Turn. (See photo opposite.)

Row 3: Ch1, 1dc same st as ch1, ch3, sk next sc, vst in next sc, ch3, *sk next sc, 1sc in next 5sc, ch3, sk next sc, vst in next sc, ch3* rep from * to * across, ending with 1dc in last sc. Turn. (See photo opposite.)

(*Note:* for row 3 you want to make sure you start with a vst and end with a vst for all sizes, adjust skipped sts as needed.)

Row 4: Ch1, 1dc in same st as ch1, ch3, 7dc in vst, ch3, *sk next sc, 1sc in next 3sc, ch3, sk next sc, 7dc in vst, ch3* rep from * to * across, ending with 1dc in last dc. Turn. (See photo opposite.)

Row 5: Ch1, 1dc in same st as ch1, ch3, 1dc (ch1, 1dc) x 6, ch3, *sk next sc, 1sc in next sc, sk next sc, ch3, 1dc (ch1, 1dc) x 6, ch3* rep from * to* across, ending with 1dc in last dc. Fasten off and weave in ends. (See photo opposite.)

Row 6: Attach Lime to where you fastened off, ch1, 1sc in same st as joining, (ch3, 1sc in next ch1sp,) rep across working only in the ch1sps. Fasten off and weave in ends. (See photo opposite.)

Sew buttons on securely.

Cappy the Cape Cod "Lobstah" Cocoon and Hat

If you are a New Englander, you know the meaning of "lobstah." If you're not, now is the perfect time to get acquainted with this long standing tradition! Cappy combines the warmth and comfort of washable wool with the charm of Cape Cod. Capture the innocence of the newborn in your life with this whimsical cocoon and hat ensemble.

Yarn

Cascade 220 Superwash 3.5oz/100gr/220yds/200m/
  #4 medium weight
Colors used in pictures:
Color number 809 / Color name: Really Red x 3 skeins
Color number 871 /Color name: White x 10yds
Color number 815 / Color name: Black x 5yds

Needle

US H8/5.00mm Susan Bates hook
Yarn Needle

Gauge

Gauge: 13sc x 16sc rows = 4"

Also Needed

Polyester Fiberfil – small amount for eyes

Glossary of Abbreviations

st(s) = stitch(es)

sk = skip

slst = slip stitch

ch = chain

sc = single crochet

trc = treble crochet

hdc = half double crochet

rep from * to * = repeat between the stars

fpsc = front post single crochet = insert hook from right to left behind sc, yo, pull back through, yo, drop off last 2 loops on hook

trc = treble crochet = yo twice, insert hook into next st, bring yarn back through, yo, drop off first 2loops, yo, drop off next 2 loops, yo, drop off last 2 loops

sc dec= sc decrease: insert hook, pull up a loop, insert hook in next stitch, pull up a loop, yo and draw through all 3 loops on hook

Finished size

Fits babies 0–2 months = 20" circumference, 27" long

COCOON

(Note: See Cappy the Cape Cod "Lobstah" Cocoon and Hat stitches p. 62)

Measures approx 20" circumference x 22" length

Start at bottom of cocoon

Row 1: With H hook and Really Red, ch2, 3sc in 2nd ch from hook, ch1, turn. (3sc). (See Fig 1 on p. 62.)

Row 2: 2sc in each sc across. Ch1, turn. (6sc)

Row 3: 2sc in first sc, 1 sc in next 4sc, 2sc in last sc. Ch1, turn. (8sc)

Row 4: 2sc in first sc, 1sc in next 6sc, 2sc in last sc. Ch1, turn. (10sc)

TAIL FINS

Row 1: 1sc in next sc, (ch4, 3trc, ch4, sc) all in same sc. sk next sc, (sc, ch4, 3trc, ch4, sc) all in next sc, sk next sc, (sc, ch4, 5trc, ch4, sc) all in next sc, sk next sc, (sc, ch4, 3trc, ch4, sc) all in next sc, sk next sc, (sc, ch4, 3trc, ch4, sc) all in next sc. (5 tail fins) Do not turn, but continue on to work in ends of rows. (See Fig 2 on p. 62.)

BODY

Rnd 1: Working across the ends of rows from rows 1–4, work 10sc into those ends of rows, (4sc around the ch4 on first tail fin, 1sc in next 3trc, 4sc around the next ch4,) repeat one more time. 5sc around the next ch4, 1sc in each of the next 5trc, 5sc around the next ch4, then repeat between the parenthesis for the last 2 fins. Slst in next sc.

Rnd 2: Ch1, 1sc in same st as joining, 1sc in next 9sc. Slst into first sc to form a circle. (10sc). (See Fig 3 on p. 62.)

Rnd 3: 2sc in same sc as joining, 1sc in next sc, *2sc in next sc, 1sc in next sc* rep from * to * around. Work in continuous rnds. (15sc)

Rnd 4: *1sc in next 2sc, 2sc in next sc* rep from * to * around. (20sc)

Rnd 5: 1fpsc around each sc around. (20fpsc). (See Fig 4 on p. 62.)

Rnd 6: Working behind the fpsc from rnd 5, 1sc in each st around. (20sc)

Rnd 7: *1sc in next 3sc, 2sc in next sc* rep from * to * around. (25sc)

Rnd 8: 1sc in each sc around. (25sc)

Rnd 9: 1fpsc around each sc around. (25fpsc)

Rnd 10: Working behind each fpsc, 1sc in each st around. (25sc)

Rnd 11: *1sc in next 4sc, 2sc in next sc* rep from * to* around. (30sc)

Rnd 12: 1sc in each sc around. (30sc)

Rnd 13: 1fpsc around each sc around. (30fpsc)

Rnd 14: Working behind each fpsc, 1sc in each st around. (30sc)

Rnd 15: 1sc in next 5sc, *2sc in next sc* rep from * to* around. (35sc)

Rnd 16: 1sc in each sc around. (35sc)

Rnd 17: 1fpsc around each sc. (35fpsc)

Rnd 18: Working behind each fpsc, 1sc in each st around. (35sc)

Rnd 19: 1sc in next 6sc, * 2sc in next sc* rep from * to* around. (40sc)

Rnd 20: *1sc in next 7sc, 2sc in next sc* rep from * to * around. (45sc)

Rnd 21: *1sc in next 8sc, 2sc in next sc* rep from * to * around. (50sc)

Rnd 22: *1sc in next 9sc, 2sc in next sc* rep from * to * around. (55sc)

Rnd 23: *1sc in next 10sc, 2sc in next sc* rep from * to * around. (60sc)

Rnd 24: *1sc in next 11sc, 2sc in next sc* rep from * to * around. (65sc)

Rnd 25: *1sc in next 12sc, 2sc in next sc* rep from * to * around. (70sc)

Rnd 26: 1sc in each sc around. (70sc)

Rnd 27: 1fpsc around each sc. (70fpsc)

Rnd 28: Working behind each fpsc, 1sc in each st around. (70sc)

Rnds 29–62: 1sc in each sc around. (70sc) or until cocoon measures approx 12" from rnd 18 to rnd 62.

Rnds 63–64: 1sc in each sc around and at the same time dec 2sc anywhere on this rnd. (66sc)

Rnd 65: 1sc in each sc around. (66sc)

Rnd 66: 1sc in next 11sc, ch11, skip next 11sc, 1sc in the next 22sc, ch11, skip next 11sc, 1sc in next 11sc.

Rnd 67: 1sc in next 11sc, 11sc around next 11chs, 1sc in next 22sc, 11sc around next 11chs, 1sc in next 11sc. (66sc)

Rnd 68: *1sc in next 9sc, sc tog the next 2sc* rep from * to * around. (60sc)

Rnd 69: *1sc in next 8sc, sc tog the next 2sc* rep from * to * around. (54sc)

Rnd 70: 1sc in each sc around. (54sc)

Rnd 71: 1fpsc around each sc around. (54fpsc)

Rnd 72: working behind the fpsc from rnd 71 *1sc in each st around. Slst to join. (54sc)

Fasten off and tie in ends.

ARMS
make 2

Rnd 1: With Really Red and H hook, attach yarn to bottom of armhole, sc in the sts around the hole working it out so you have 22sc. (22sc) Work in continuous rnds.

Rnd 2: 1sc in each sc around. (22sc)

Rnd 3: 1fpsc around each sc around. (22fpsc)

Rnd 4: working in the back of rnd 3, 1sc in each st around. (22sc)

Rnds 5–7: 1sc in each sc around. (22sc)

Rnd 8: 1fpsc around each sc around. (22fpsc)

Rnd 9: Working in the back of rnd 8, 1sc in each st around. (22sc)

Rnd 10: *1sc in next 10sc, 2sc in next sc* repeat fro * to * once more. (24sc)

Rnd 11: 1sc in next 11sc, 2sc in next sc, 1sc in next 12sc. (25sc)

Rnd 12: 1sc in each of the next 15sc, skip next 10sc, slst to join to form a circle. (15sc)

Notes: you might want to play around with this round so that you can get your 15sc in the right position. You want to fold the arm in half and look for 15sc that position the claw as shown in pictures. The 15sc are going to be at the top and the 10sc that you skip will later form the bottom claw. So you want to find the top middle stitch. And count 7sc after you find the middle stitch, then skip 10sc and slst to join.

LARGE CLAW ON TOP
Rnd 1: 1sc in each sc around. (15sc). (See Fig 5 on p. 62.)

Rnd 2: 2sc in next sc, 1sc in next 6sc, skip next sc, sc in next sc, skip next sc, 1sc in next 4, 2sc in last sc. (15sc)

Rnds 3–10: Repeat rnd 2 (15sc)

Rnd 11: 1sc in next 8sc, ch1, turn. Sc through both thickness to close top of claw. (See Fig 6 on p. 62.)

Fasten off and weave in ends.

SMALL CLAW ON BOTTOM
Rnd1: Sk first unworked sc and attach to next unworked sc on rnd 12, 1sc in next 9sc. Work in continuous rnds. (10sc). (See Fig 7 on p. 62.)

Rnd 2: Sk next sc, 1sc in each sc around. (9sc)

Rnd 3: 2sc in first sc, 1sc in next 2sc, skip next sc, 1sc in next sc, skip next sc, 1sc in next 2sc, 2sc in last sc. (9sc)

Rnds 4–7: Repeat rnd 3.

Rnd 8: 1sc in next 5sc, working through both thickness sc the top of the claw tog. Fasten off and weave in ends. (See Fig 8 on p. 62.)

Repeat for second arm.

"LOBSTAH" HAT
measures approx 14.5" circumference, approx 5" long

Rnd 1: With Really Red and H hook, ch2, 6sc in 2nd ch from hook. (6sc) Work in continuous rnds.

Rnd 2: 2sc in each sc around. (12sc)

Rnd 3: *1sc in next sc, 2sc in next sc* rep from * to * around. (18sc)

Rnd 4: *1sc in next 2sc, 2sc in next sc* rep from * to * around. (24sc)

Rnd 5: 1sc in the next 5sc, 1sc in the front loop of the next sc, ch20, 1hdc in 3rd ch from hook, 1sc in next ch, 1slst in remaining chs, 1sc in each of the next 11sc, 1sc in the front loop of the next sc, ch20, 1hdc in 3rd ch from hook, 1sc in next ch, 1slst in remaining chs, 1sc in last 6sc. (24sc)

Cappy the Cape Cod "Lobstah" Cocoon and Hat stitches

(Fig 1) row 1 tail. (See p. 60.)

(Fig 2) tail fins. (See p. 60.)

(Fig 3) rnd 2 of body. (See p. 60.)

(Fig 4) fpsc on body. (See p. 60.)

(Fig 5) rnd one of claw. (See p. 61.)

(Fig 6) closing first large claw. (See p. 61.)

(Fig 7) starting small bottom claw. (See p. 61.)

(Fig 8) both claws. (See p. 61.)

Rnd 6: 1sc in each sc around and 1sc behind each antenna. (24sc)

Rnd 7: *1sc in next 3sc, 2sc in next sc* rep from * to * around. (30sc)

Rnd 8: *1sc in next 4sc, 2sc in next sc* rep from * to * around. (36sc)

Rnd 9: *1sc in next 5sc, 2sc in next sc* rep from * to * around. (42sc)

Rnd 10: *1sc in next 6sc, 2sc in next sc* rep from * to * around. (48sc)

Rnds 11–17: 1sc in each sc around. (48sc)

Rnd 18: 1sc in next 3sc, *sc tog the next 2sc, 1sc in next 3sc* rep from * to * around. (39sc)

Rnd 19: 1sc in each sc around. (39sc)

Rnd 20: 1fpsc around each sc around. (39fpsc) (Make sure hat measures approx 5" after this rnd.)

Row 1: Forming earflaps and ties: Working in the loops behind the fpsc from rnd 17, 1sc in each of the next 15sc, ch1, turn. Leave the rest of the row unworked for now. Ch1, turn.

Rows 2–3: 1sc in next 7sc. Ch1, turn. (7sc)

Row 4: Sc first 2sc tog, 1sc in next 3sc, sc last 2sc tog. Ch1, turn. (5sc)

Row 5: 1sc in next 5sc. Ch1, turn. (5sc)

Row 6: Sc first 2sc tog, 1sc in next sc, sc last 2sc tog. Ch1, turn. (3sc)

Row 7: Sc the next 3sc tog. Ch 35, slst in 2nd ch from hook, 1slst in each of the remaining chs, slst into same st as beg. Slst down left side of earflap to row 1.

Row 1: 1sc in each of the next 20sc, ch1 turn. Leave the rest of the row unworked for now.

Rows 2–7: Repeat rows 2–7 of first earflap.

Then finish Row 1: 1sc in each of the last 4sc on row 1, slst to join. Fasten off and tie in ends.

EYEBALLS
make 2

Rnd 1: With Black and H hook, ch 2, 8sc in 2nd ch from hook. Slst to join. (8sc) Fasten off Black and attach White.

Rnd 2: 2sc in each sc around. (16sc)

Rnd 3: 1sc in next sc, *sc tog the next 2sc, 1sc in next sc* rep from * to * around. Slst to join. (11sc) Fasten off, leaving a tail to sew with. Stuff eyeballs and attach them to top of hat as shown in pictures. Weave in all ends.

Maryjane Booties

Your sweet little baby girl will be warm and stylish in these adorable Maryjane booties. Frilly and fanciful, this throwback never goes out of style.

Yarn
Cascade Superwash 220 3.5oz/100g/220yds/200m/
  #4 medium weight
Colors used in pictures:
Color number 1941 / Color name: Salmon x 2oz
Color number 871 / Color name: White x 1oz

Needle
US G6/4.00mm Susan Bates hook
Yarn needle

Gauge
15sc x 18sc = 4"

Also Needed
Satin roses x 2

Glossary of Abbreviations
st(s) = stitch(es)
slst = slip stitch
rnd(s) = round(s)
tog = together
BL = Back loop(s)
FL = front loop(s)
ch = chain
sc = single crochet
hdc = half double crochet

Finished Sizes
0–3 months = 3" sole
3–6 months = 3.5" sole
6–12 months = 4" sole
12–18 months = 4.5" sole
18–24 months = 5" sole
Instructions are written 0–3, other sizes are in parenthesis

BOOTIE

make 2

Rnd 1: With desired color, ch7 (ch8, ch9, ch10, ch11), 3sc in 2nd ch from hook, 1sc in next 4ch (5ch, 6ch, 7ch, 8ch), 6sc in last ch. Now working on opposite side of ch, 1sc in next 4ch (5ch, 6ch, 7ch, 8ch). Slst to join. (17sc, 19sc, 21sc, 23sc, 25sc). (Fig 1 opposite refers to Rnds 1–4.)

Rnd 2: Ch1, 2sc in same st as joining, 2sc in next 2sc, 1sc in next 4sc (5sc, 6sc, 7sc, 8sc), 2sc in next 6sc, 1sc in next 4sc (5sc, 6sc, 7sc, 8sc). Slst to join rnd. (26sc, 28sc, 30sc, 32sc, 34sc)

Rnd 3: Ch1, 2sc in same st as joining, (1sc in next sc, 2sc in next sc) x 2, 1sc in next 5sc (6sc, 7sc, 8sc, 9sc), (2sc in next sc, 1sc in next sc) x 6, 1sc in next 4sc (5sc, 6sc, 7sc, 8sc). Slst to join rnd. (35sc, 37sc, 39sc, 41sc, 43sc)

Rnd 4: Ch1, 1sc in the BL of each sc around. Slst to join rnd. (35sc, 37sc, 39sc, 41sc, 43sc). (See Fig 2 opposite.)

Rnd 5: Ch1, 1hdc in same st as joining, 1hdc in next 15sc (16sc, 17sc, 18sc, 19sc), (hdc tog the next 2sc, 1hdc in next sc) x 5, 1hdc in next 4sc (5sc, 6sc, 7sc, 8sc). Slst to join rnd. (30hdc, 32hdc, 34hdc, 36hdc, 38hdc). (See Fig 3 opposite.)

Rnd 6: Ch1, 1hdc in same st as joining, 1hdc in next 15hdc (16hdc, 17hdc, 18hdc, 19hdc), (hdc tog the next 2hdc, 1hdc in next hdc) x 4, 1hdc in next 2hdc (3hdc, 4hdc, 5hdc, 6hdc). Slst to join rnd. (26hdc, 28hdc, 30hdc, 32hdc, 34hdc)

Rnd 7: Ch1, 1sc in same st as joining, 1sc in next 14hdc (15hdc, 16hdc, 17hdc, 18hdc), (hdc tog the next 2sts) x 4, 1sc in next 3hdc (4hdc, 5hdc, 6hdc, 7hdc). Slst to join rnd. (22sts, 24sts, 26sts, 28sts, 30sts). (See Fig 4 opposite.)

Rnd 8: Ch1, 1sc in same st as joining, 1sc in each st around. Slst to join rnd. (22sc, 24sc, 26sc, 28sc, 30sc)

Rnd 9: Ch1, 1sc in same st as joining, 1sc in next 11sc (13sc, 15sc, 17sc, 19sc), ch6, skipping 9sc (10sc, 11sc, 12sc, 13sc) on toe, 1slst in first sc. (See Fig 5 opposite.)

Rnd 10: Ch1, 1sc in same st as joining, 1sc in each sc and in each ch around. Slst to join rnd. (18 sc, 20sc, 22sc, 24sc, 26sc) Fasten off and weave in ends. (See Fig 6 opposite.)

Ruffles on Bottom of Bootie

With White and with opening of bootie facing you, attach yarn in any FL from rnd 4 that was created when you made the BL, ch2, 1hdc in same loop, *sk next loop, (slst in next loop, ch2, 1hdc) all in same loop* rep from * to * around. Slst to join rnd. Fasten off and weave in ends.

Ruffles on Top of Bootie

With White, attach yarn to any sc on top of bootie, ch2, 1hdc in same sc, *sk next sc, (slst in next sc, ch2, 1hdc) all in same sc* rep from * to * around. Slst to join rnd. Fasten off and weave in ends.

White Ruffle on Toe of Bootie

Rnd 1: With White, ch2, 8sc in 2nd ch from hook. Slst to join rnd. (8sc)

Rnd 2: Ch2, 1hdc in same st as joining *(slst in next sc, ch2, 1hdc) all in same st* rep from * to* around. Slst to join. Fasten off and weave in ends.

Sew satin flower in center of white ruffle. Sew white ruffle to top of toe as seen inpictures.

Maryjane Booties stitches

(Fig 1) rnds 1-4 sole. See opposite.

(Fig 2) working in backloops (BL). See rnd 4 opposite.

(Fig 3) hdc's decreases on toes. See rnd 5 opposite.

(Fig 4) forming toes. See rnd 7 opposite.

(Fig 5) rnd 9 strap formed. See opposite.

(Fig 6) rnd 10 strap. See opposite.

Owl Afghan

Don't wake the owls! Your baby will enjoy year-round comfort swaddled in this adorable owl afghan. Whether out for a stroll or taking a nap, these sleeping owls will provide hours of peaceful slumber for the loved one in your life.

Yarn

Cascade Pinwheel 7oz/200g/440yds/400m/#4 medium weight

Colors used in pictures:

Color number 04 / Color name: Easter Eggs x 2 skeins

Cascade 220 Superwash 3.5oz/100g/220yds/200m/ #4 medium weight

Colors used in pictures:

Color number 871 / Color name: White x 3 skeins

Color number 851 / Color name: Lime x 1 skeins

Color number 849 / Color name: Dark Aqua x 1 skein

Color number 820 / Color name: Lemon x 1oz

Needle

US H8/5.00mm Susan Bates hook

Sewing thread

Sewing needle

Yarn needle

Gauge

12sc x 13sc rows = 4"

Glossary of Abbreviations

st(s) = stitch(es)	rnd(s) = round(s)
slst = slip stitch	dc = double crochet
sk = skip	hdc = half double crochet
RS = right side	rep from * to *= repeat from * to *
WS = wrong side	sp = space
chsp = chain space	ch2 counts as 1hdc
ch = chain	ch3 counts as 1dc
sc = single crochet	ch4 counts as 1trc

beg corner st = (ch3, 2dc, ch1, 3dc) all in same sp as attached

corner st = (3dc, ch1, 3dc) all in next ch1sp

feather st = work 5dc up first post of first dc, ch2, work 5dc down 2nd post of next dc

Finished Size

Afghan measures 36" x 42"

OWL SQUARE
(Note: See Owl Afghan stitches p. 73)

Make 6

Rnd 1: With Easter Egg and H hook, make a magic circle (see p. 4), work 6sc inside circle, pull circle tight. Work in continuous rnds. (6sc)

Rnd 2: 2sc in each sc around. (12sc)

Rnd 3: 2sc in each sc around. (24sc)

Rnd 4: 1sc in each sc around. (24sc)

Rnd 5: *1sc in next sc, 2sc in next sc* rep from * to * around. (36sc)

Rnd 6: 1sc in each sc around. (36sc)

Rnd 7: *1sc in next 2sc, 2sc in next sc* rep from * to * around. (48sc) Fasten off and weave in ends.

Rnd 8: Attach Dark Aqua to where you fastened off, ch2, 1hdc in next 11sc, work (1hdc, 2dc, 1trc, ch2, 1slst in top of trc, 2dc, 1hdc) all in the front loop of next sc (1st ear), 1sc in next 11sc, (1hdc, 2dc, 1trc, ch2, 1slst in top of trc, 2dc, 1hdc) all in the front loop of next sc (2nd ear), 1hdc in next 23sc. slst to ch2 to join rnd. Fasten off and weave in ends. (See Figs 1 and 2 on p. 73.)

Rnd 9: With White and H hook, attach yarn in stitch behind 1st ear, ch1, 1sc in same st as joining, 1sc in next 11sc, 1sc behind 2nd ear, 1sc in next 34sts. Slst to join rnd. (48sc). (See Fig 3 on p. 73. Fig 4 on p. 73 refers to rnds 9–12.)

Rnd 10: Ch3, 2dc in same st as joining, ch1, 3dc in same st as joining, 1dc in next 11sc, *(3dc, ch1, 3dc) in next sc, 1dc in next 11sc* rep from * to * around. Slst to join rnd. (68dc)

Rnd 11: Ch3, 1dc in next 2dc, (3dc, ch1, 3dc) in next ch1sp, *1dc in next 17dc, (3dc, ch1, 3dc) in next ch1sp* rep from * to * 2 more times, 1dc in next 14dc. Slst to join rnd. (92dc)

Rnd 12: Ch1, 1sc in same st as joining, 1sc in each dc around working 2sc in each ch1sp in the corners. Slst to join rnd. (100sc)

Fasten off and weave in ends.

WHITES OF EYES
make 12

Rnd 1: With F hook and White, make a magic circle (see p. 4), 6sc inside circle, pull circle closed. (6sc) Work in continuous rnds.

Rnd 2: 2sc in each sc around. (12sc)

Rnd 3: *1sc in next, 2sc in next sc* rep from * to * around. (18sc)

Fasten off leaving a tail to sew with. Embroider black sleepy eyes onto whites of eyes. Then sew eyes onto face of owl.

BEAK
make 6

Row 1: With F hook and yellow, ch2, 1sc in 2nd ch from hook. Turn. (1sc)

Row 2: 2sc in sc. Turn. (2sc)

Row 3: 2sc in next 2sc. (4sc) Do not turn. Now work around entire beak.

Rnd 1: working 2sc in each corner of triangle, and working 1sc in each end of row. Work sc all around rows 1–3.

Fasten off leaving a tail to sew with.

Sew nose under eyes.

JUST CIRCLE SQUARES
make 10
Repeat rnds 1–7 of owl square. Fasten off and weave in ends.

Rnd 8: With Lime Green and H hook, attach yarn to where you fastened off. Ch3, 1hdc in each sc around. Slst to join rnd. (48hdc)

Fasten off and weave in ends.

Rnd 9: With White and H hook, attach yarn where you fastened off, ch1, 1sc in same st as joining, 1sc in each hdc around. Slst to join rnd. (48sc)

Rnd 10: Ch3, 2dc in same st as joining, ch1, 3dc in same st as joining, 1dc in next 11sc, *(3dc, ch1, 3dc) in next sc, 1dc in next 11sc* rep from * to * around. (68dc)

Rnd 11: Ch3, 1dc in next 2dc, (3dc, ch1, 3dc) in next ch1sp, *1dc in next 17dc, (3dc, ch1, 3dc) in next ch1sp* rep from * to * 2 more times, 1dc in next 14dc. Slst to join rnd. (92dc)

Rnd 12: Ch1, 1sc in same st as joining, 1sc in each dc around working 2sc in each ch1sp in the corners. Slst to join rnd. (100sc)

MIDDLE OF AFGHAN

Row 1: (WS) With Pinwheel and H hook, ch58, 1dc in 4th ch from hook, ch1, sk next 2 ch, 2dc in next ch, *ch1, sk next 2ch, 2dc in next ch* rep from * to* across. Turn. (19 groups of 2dc) (see picture 1). (See Fig 5 on p. 73.)

Row 2: (RS) Ch3, work 5 dc down post of next dc, ch2, work 5 dc up post of 2nd dc, ch1, sk next 2dc, *work 5 dc down post of next dc, ch2, work 5 dc up post of next dc, ch1, sk next 2dc* – feather st made. Rep from * to * to ending with 1dc in last dc. Turn. (9 feathers). (See Figs 6–8 on p. 73.)

Row 3: Ch 3, 2dc in between 2dc from previous base rnd, ch1, 2dc in middle sp of first feather, ch1, *2dc in between 2dc from previous base rnd, ch1, 2dc in middle of next feather, ch1* rep from * to * across ending with 1dc in last dc. Turn (18 groups of 2dc). (See Fig 9 on p. 73.)

Row 4: Slst over to 2nd set of 2dc, *feather st around next 2dc, ch1, sk next 2dc*. Rep from * to * across, ending with 1dc in last dc. Turn. (9 feathers). (See Fig 10 on p. 73.)

Row 5: Ch3, 2dc in middle of next feather, ch1, 2dc in between 2dc from previous base rnd, ch1, *2dc in middle of next feather, ch1, 2dc in between 2dc from previous base rnd, ch1* rep from * to * across ending with 1dc in last dc. Turn. (18 groups of 2dc)

Row 6: Ch1, slst in next ch1sp from previous row, *feather st around next 2dc, ch1, sk next 2dc* rep from * to * across, ending with 1dc in last dc. Turn. (9 feathers)

Row 7: Ch3, 2dc in between 2dc from previous base rnd, ch1, 2dc in middle of next feather, ch1 *2dc in between 2dc from previous base rnd, ch1, 2dc in middle of next feather, ch1* rep from * to * across ending with 1dc in last dc. Turn. (18 groups of 2dc)

Row 8: Slst over to 2nd set of 2dc, *feather st around next 2dc, ch1, sk next 2dc*, Rep from * to * across, ending with 1dc in last dc. Turn. (9 feathers)

Row 9: Ch3, 2dc in middle of next feather, ch1, 2dc in between 2dc from previous base rnd, ch1, *2dc in middle of next feather, ch1, 2dc in between 2dc from previous base rnd, ch1* rep from * to * across ending with 1dc in last dc. Turn. (18 groups of 2dc)

Row 10: Ch1, slst in next ch1sp from previous row, *feather st around next 2dc, ch1, sk next 2dc* rep from * to * across, ending with 1dc in last dc. Turn. (9 feathers)

Rows 11 – 62: repeat rows 3–10 in sequence.

Next: Sew 4 squares x 5 squares around middle of afghan to join the squares to the middle section of the afghan, as shown in pictures.

BORDER

Rnd 1: With White, work 1sc in each end of row around entire afghan. Work it so that you have 50sts on the top row and bottom row and 75sts on each long side. Slst to join.

Rnd 2: Ch3, 1dc in each sc around, working (3dc, ch1, 3dc) in each of the 4 corners on afghan. Slst to join.

Rnd 3: Ch3, 1dc in each dc around, working (1dc, ch1, 1dc) in each of the 4 corners. Slst to join. Fasten off White and weave in ends.

Rnd 4: Attach Green to where you fastened off, 1dc in each dc around, working (1dc, ch1, 1dc) in each of the 4 corners on afghan. Slst to join. Fasten off and weave in ends.

Rnd 5: Attach White where you fastened off, ch3, 1dc in each sc around, working (1dc, ch1, 1dc) in each of the 4 corners on afghan. Slst to join.

Rnd 6: Ch3, 1dc in each dc around, working (1dc, ch1, 1dc) in each of the 4 corners. Slst to join. Fasten off White and weave in ends.

Rnd 7: Attach Dark Aqua where you fastened off, ch3, 1dc in each dc around, working (1dc, ch1, 1dc) in each of the 4 corners on afghan. Slst to join. Fasten off and weave in ends.

Rnd 8: Attach White where you fastened off, ch3, 1dc in each dc around, working (1dc, ch1, 1dc) in each of the 4 corners on afghan. Slst to join. Fasten off. Weave in ends.

FEATHERS BORDER

Rnd 1: With Pinwheel, attach yarn to any corner st, *5dc down next dc, ch2, 5dc up next dc, sk next 3dc* rep from * to * around making sure to work it out so that you have a feather in each corner. Slst to join rnd.

Rnd 2: Ch1, 1sc in each st around, working in ends of rows and in middle of feathers and in stitch in between feathers. Slst to join rnd. Fasten off and weave in ends.

Owl Afghan stitches

(Fig 1) 1st owl ear. (See rnd 8 on p. 70.)

(Fig 2) 2nd owl ear. (See rnd 8 on p. 70.)

(Fig 3) working behind owl ear. (See rnd 9 on p. 70.)

(Fig 4) completed background of owl square. (See rnds 9–12 on p. 70.)

(Fig 5) foundation row. (See p. 71.)

(Fig 6) 5dc around 1st dc. (See row 2 p. 71.)

(Fig 7) 5 dc up next dc post. (See row 2 p. 71.)

(Fig 8) 1st row of feathers. (See row 2 p. 71.)

(Fig 9) 2nd foundation row. (See row 3 on p. 71.)

(Fig 10) 2nd feather row. alternate feathers. (See row 4 on p. 71.)

Owl Costume

Give a hoot! Your little feathered friend will look so cute! Imaginative and wondrous, this whimsical owl costume is a must-have for your photo mementos.

Yarn

Cascade 220 Superwash 3.5oz/100grams/220yds/ #4 medium weight

Colors used in pictures:

Color number 871 / Color name: White x 3 skeins

Color number 802 / Color name: Green Apple x 1 skein

Color Number 849 / Color name: Dark Aqua x 2oz

Color number 821 / Color name: Daffodil x 3oz

Needle

US F5/3.75mm Susan Bates hook

US G6/4.00mm Susan Bates hook

US H8/5.00mm Susan Bates hook

US I9/5.50mm Susan Bates hook

Yarn needle

Gauge

H hook = 12sc x 13sc rows = 4"

Glossary of Abbreviations

rnd(s) = round(s)

sk = skip

trc = treble crochet

BL = back loop

RS = right side

yo = yarn over hook

sc = single crochet

dc = double crochet

slst = slip stitch

vst = v stitch = 1dc, ch1, 1dc

ch = chain

hdc = half double crochet

dtrc = double treble crochet = yo3times, yo, drop off 2loops three times.

rep from * to * = repeat between the stars

feather st = work 5dc up first post of first dc, ch2, work 5dc down 2nd post of next dc

fpsc = front post single crochet = insert hook from right to left behind sc, yo, pull back through, yo, drop off last 2 loops on hook

Finished Sizes

0–6 months, 12–18 months, and 24 months

Please make sure to check your gauge to mine. I tend to crochet loose, so you might need to go up a few hook sizes to make your outfit match my gauge.

To make owl body use G hook = 0–6 months, H hook = 12–18 months, I hook = 24 months

To make hats use H hook for all sizes

To make booties/legwarmers use H hook for all sizes

OWL BODY

(Note: See Owl Costume stitches p. 83)
0–6 months = 14" neck to crotch
12–18 months = 15" neck to crotch
24 months = 16" neck to crotch

Start at crotch.

Rnd 1: With G, H or I hook and White, ch2, 6sc in 2nd ch from hook. (6sc) Work in continuous rnds. Use a placemarker if desired to keep your place.

Rnd 2: 2sc in each sc around. (12sc)

Rnd 3: 2sc in each sc around. (24sc)

Rnd 4: *1sc in next sc, 2sc in next sc* rep from * to * around. (36sc)

Rnd 5: *1sc in next 2sc, 2sc in next sc* rep from * to * around. (48sc)

Rnd 6: 1sc in each sc around. (48sc)

Rnd 7: 1sc in next 2sc, ch 30, sk next 20sc, (leg opening) 1sc in next 4sc, ch30, sk next 20sc, 1sc in next 2sc. (See Fig 1 on p. 83.)

Note: working around the chain instead of working in each chain will allow more stretch for the leg opening. (See Fig 2 on p. 83.)

Rnd 8: 1sc in next 2sc, 30sc around chains, 1sc in next 4sc, 30sc around chains, 1sc in next 2sc. (68sc)

Rnd 9: 1sc in next 2sc, *2sc in next sc, 1sc in next 2sc* rep from * to * around. Slst in next sc. (90sc)

Rnd 10: Base Rnd: Ch3, 1dc in same st as joining, ch2, sk next 2sc, *2dc in next sc, ch2, sk next 2sc* rep from * to * around. Slst to join rnd. (30 groups of 2dc). (See Fig 3 on p. 83.)

Rnd 11: Ch1, 5dc around the post of 1st dc, ch2, 5dc around the post of the 2nd dc, (feather st) ch1, sk next 2dc *5dc around the post of the next dc, ch2, 5dc around the post of the 2nd dc, ch1, sk next 2dc* rep from * to * around. Slst into middle of next feather to join rnd. (15 feathers). (See Figs 4 and 5 on p. 83.)

Rnd 12: Ch3, 1dc in same sp as joining, ch2 *2dc in between 2dc from previous base rnd, ch2, 2dc in middle of next feather, ch2* rep from * to * around. Slst to dc to join rnd. (30 groups of 2dc)

Rnd 13: Ch1, slst in next dc, 2ch and next dc, ch1, turn so opening of costume is facing your right hand, 5dc around 1st dc post, ch2, turn your work the other way so that the opening of the costume is facing your left hand, 5dc around post of next dc, ch1, *sk next 2dc, 5dc around the post of the next dc, ch2, 5dc around the post of the 2nd dc, ch1* rep from * to * around. Slst in middle of next feather to join rnd.

Next: Repeat rnds 12 and 13 alternately, until body measures approx to underarms 9" (10", 12") or to desired length. Fasten off and weave in ends.

Note: the next 8 rows of the panels are going to make the arm openings and slit in back.

Right Back Panel

Row 1: Find the middle of the back of costume, working from the inside of costume, attach White to the middle of a feather, ch4, 2dc in middle of next feather, ch1, *2dc in between 2dc from previous base row, ch1, 2dc in middle of next feather, ch1* rep from * to * 2 more times, 1dc in middle of next feather. Turn. (7 groups of 2dc)

Note: you want to make sure to stagger your feathers just like you did for the body. Continue in established pattern as for body.

Row 2: (RS) Ch1, work 5 dc down post of next dc, ch2, work 5 dc up post of 2nd dc, ch1, *sk next 2dc, work 5 dc down post of next dc, ch2, work 5 dc up post of next dc, ch1* rep from * to * across, ending with 1dc in last dc. Turn. (4 feathers)

Row 3: Ch 3, 2dc in middle sp of next feather, ch1, *2dc in between 2dc from previous base rnd, ch1, 2dc in middle of next feather, ch1* rep from * to * across, ending with 1dc in last dc. Turn. (7 groups of 2dc)

Row 4: Ch1, slst over 5sts, *feather st around next 2dc, ch1, sk next 2dc* rep from * to * across, ending with 1dc in last dc. Turn. (3 feathers)

Row 5: Ch3, 2dc in between 2dc from previous base rnd, ch1, *2dc in middle of next feather, ch1, 2dc in between 2dc from previous base rnd, ch1* rep from * to * across ending with 1dc in last dc. Turn. (7 groups of 2dc)

Row 6: Ch3, *feather st around next 2dc, ch1, sk next 2dc* rep from * to * across, ending with 1dc in last dc. Turn. (4 feathers)

Row 7: Ch3, 2dc in middle of next feather, ch1* 2dc in between 2dc from previous base rnd, ch1, 2dc in middle of next feather, ch1* rep from * to * across ending with 1dc in last dc. Turn. (7 groups of 2dc)

Row 8: Ch1, slst over 5sts, *feather st around next 2dc, ch1, sk next 2dc* rep from * to * across, ending with 1dc in last dc. Turn. (3 feathers)

Row 9: Ch3, 2dc in between 2dc from previous base rnd, ch1, *2dc in middle of next feather, ch1, 2dc in between 2dc from previous base rnd, ch1* rep from * to * across ending with 1dc in last dc. Turn. (7 groups of 2dc)

Row 10: Ch3, *feather st around next 2dc, ch1, sk next 2dc* rep from * to * across, ending with 1dc in last dc. Turn. (4 feathers) Fasten off and weave in ends.

Front Panel

Row 1: With White, attach yarn in same middle of feather as right back panel. Ch3, 2dc in between 2dc from previous base rnd, ch1, *2dc in middle of next feather, ch1, 2dc in between 2dc from previous base rnd, ch1* rep from * to * 5 more times, ending with 1dc in middle of next feather. Turn. (13 groups of 2dc)

Row 2: Ch3, *feather st around next 2dc, ch1, sk next 2dc* rep from * to * across, ending with 1dc in last dc. Turn. (7 feathers)

Row 3: Ch3, * 2dc in middle of next feather, ch1, *2dc in between 2dc from previous base rnd, ch1, 2dc in middle of next feather, ch1* rep from * to * across ending with 1dc in last dc. Turn. (13 groups of 2dc)

Row 4: Ch1, slst over 5sts, *feather st around next 2dc, ch1, sk next 2dc* rep from * to * across, ending with 1dc in last dc. Turn. (6 feathers)

Row 5: Ch3, 2dc in between 2dc from previous base rnd, ch1, *2dc in middle of next feather, ch1, 2dc in between 2dc from previous base rnd, ch1* rep from * to * across ending with 1dc in last dc. Turn. (13 groups of 2dc)

Row 6: Ch3, *feather st around next 2dc, ch1, sk next 2dc* rep from * to * across, ending with 1dc in last dc. Turn. (7 feathers)

Row 7: Ch3, * 2dc in middle of next feather, ch1, *2dc in between 2dc from previous base rnd, ch1, 2dc in middle of next feather, ch1* rep from * to * across ending with 1dc in last dc. Turn. (13 groups of 2dc)

Row 8: Ch1, slst over 5sts, *feather st around next 2dc, ch1, sk next 2dc*, Rep from * to * across, ending with 1dc in last dc. Turn. (6 feathers)

Row 9: Ch3, 2dc in between 2dc from previous base rnd, ch1, *2dc in middle of next feather, ch1, 2dc in between 2dc from previous base rnd, ch1* rep from * to * across ending with 1dc in last dc. Turn. (13 groups of 2dc)

Row 10: Ch3, *feather st around next 2dc, ch1, sk next 2dc* rep from * to * across, ending with 1dc in last dc. Turn. (7 feathers) Fasten off and weave in ends.

Left Back Panel

Row 1: With White, attach yarn in between same middle feather from where your last dc was on the front panel, working in established pattern, work your base row the same as for right back panel.

Rows 2–10: Repeat rows 2–10 the same as for right back panel.

At end of row 10 do not fasten off but continue on to neck edge instructions.

Neck Edge

Note: you are going to work all the way around top of costume and in ends of rows for each arm opening and for the slit.

Rnd 1: Change to G hook, with outside of costume facing you, 1sc in each end of row on arm openings, working down one side and up the other side of the arm openings, at same time, work 1sc in each end of feather and in middle of each feather and 1sc in between each 2dcgroup. Slst to first sc to join rnd. Fasten off.

You now are going to work in rows again.

Row 1: With Blue, attach yarn to left back panel, 1sc in each sc across neck edge, skipping over the arm openings and just sc in the next sc on top of neck edge. Do not connect the back slit, leave that open. Turn.

Rows 2–3: Ch1, *1sc in next 2sc, sc tog the next 2sc* rep from * to * across neck edge. Turn.

Row 4: Ch3, 1dc in first sc, *ch2, sk next sc, 2dc in next sc* rep from * to * across neck edge. Turn.

Row 5: Working in established pattern, work feathers in every other 2dc groups. Turn.

Row 6: (1st tie) ch60, 1slst in 2nd ch from hook, 1slst in each rem ch, sc in stitches across neck edge, (2nd tie) ch60, 1slst in 2nd ch from hook, 1slst in each rem ch. Fasten off and weave in ends.

WINGS

Rnd 1: With I (J, K) hook and Green, ch2, 6sc in 2nd ch from hook. Slst to join rnd. (6sc). (See Fig 6 on p. 83 referring to rnds 1–8 of the feather.)

Note: Ch4 counts as 1dc + 1ch.

Ch2 counts as first hdc.

Rnd 2: Ch4, 1dc in same st as joining, ch1, (*vst in next sc, ch1*) rep from * to * 4 more times. Slst to 3rd ch to join rnd. (6vsts)

Rnd 3: Ch2, 1hdc in each dc and in each chsp around. Slst to join rnd. (24hdc)

Rnd 4: Ch4, 1dc in same st as joining, ch1, sk next hdc, *vst in next hdc, ch1, sk next hdc* repeat from * to *. Slst to join rnd. (12vsts)

Rnd 5: Ch2, 1hdc in each dc and in each chsp around. Slst to join rnd. (48hdc)

Rnd 6: Ch4, 1dc in same st as joining, ch1, sk next hdc, *vst in next hdc, ch1, sk next hdc* repeat from * to *. Slst to join rnd. (24vsts)

Rnd 7: Ch2, 1hdc in 45dc and chsps, 1dc in next chsp, 1trc in next dc, 3dtrc in next chsp, 1trc in next dc, 1dc in next chsp, 1hdc in next 46dc and chsps. Slst to join rnd.

Rnd 8: Ch3, 1dc in same st as joining, *sk next 3sts, (slst in next st, ch3, 1dc in same st)* rep from * to * to middle dtrc, (1sc, ch8, 1sc) in top of middle dtrc, repeat from * to * again. Slst to join rnd. Fasten off leaving a tail to sew with. (See Fig 7 on p. 83.)

BOOTIE AND LEGWARMERS

make 2

Rnd 1: With H hook and Daffodil, ch8 (ch10, ch12), (heel) 3sc in 2nd ch from hook, 1sc in next 5ch (7ch, 9ch), (toe) 5sc in last ch. Now working on opposite side of ch, 1sc in next 5ch (7ch, 9ch). Slst to join. (18sc, 22sc, 26sc)

Rnd 2: Ch1, 2sc same st as joining, 2sc in next 2sc, 1sc in next 5sc (7sc, 9sc), 2sc in next 5sc, 1sc in next 5sc (7sc, 9sc). slst to join. (26sc, 30sc, 34sc)

Rnd 3: Ch1, 2sc in same st as joining, (1sc in next sc, 2sc in next sc) x 2, 1sc in next 6sc (8sc, 10sc), (2sc in next sc, 1sc in next sc) x 5, 1sc in next 5sc (7sc, 9sc). Slst to join. (34sc, 38sc, 42sc)

Rnd 4: Ch1, 1sc in BL of same st as joining, 1sc in BL of each sc around. slst to join. (34sc, 38sc, 42sc)

Rnd 5: Ch1, 1sc in same st as joining, 1sc in each sc around. Slst to join. (34sc, 38sc, 42sc)

Rnd 6: Ch1, 1sc in same st as joining, 1sc in next 14sc (16sc, 18sc), (1dc in next 5sc, slst in next sc) x 2, 1dc in next 5sc, 1sc in next 2sc (4sc, 6sc). Slst to join. (34sts, 38sts, 42sts). (See Figs 8, 9, 10 on p. 83)

Rnd 7: Ch1, 1sc in same st as joining, 1sc in next 14sc, (16sc, 18sc), (5dc cluster, slst in next slst) x 2, 5dc cluster, 1sc in next 2sc (4sc, 6sc). Slst to join. (22sc, 26sc, 30sc)

Rnd 8: Ch1, 1sc in each st around. When you get to the slst in between toes, work 1sc under slst of rnd 6. Do not slst to join, but now work in continuous rnds.

Note: to position your stitches in the back of the leg, 1sc in next 6sc. Adjust your stitches as you work the leg so that the stitch change seam stays in the back of the legs.
On all the rnds are after you finish a fpsc rnd, you work all the sc under the two loops that are behind the fpsc. Working increases as indicated on rnds.

Rnd 9–12: 1sc in each sc around. (22sc, 26sc, 30sc)

Rnd 13: 1fpsc around each sc around.

Rnd 14: 1sc in each sc around and at the same time increase rnd by 2sts. (24sc, 28sc, 32sc)

Rnds 15–16: 1sc in each sc around. (24sc, 28sc, 32sc)

Rnd 17: 1fpsc around each sc around. (24fpsc, 28fpsc, 32fpsc)

Rnd 18: 1sc in each sc around and at the same time increase rnd by 2sts. (26sc, 30sc, 34sc)

Rnds 19–20: 1sc in each sc around. (26sc, 30sc, 34sc)

Rnd 21: 1fpsc around each sc around. (26fpsc, 30fpsc, 34fpsc)

Rnds 22–24: 1sc in each st around. (26sc, 30sc, 34sc)

Rnds 25–44, (Rnds 25–48, Rnds 25–52): repeat rnds 21–24 in sequence. Fasten off and weave in ends.

HAT

Note: instructions are written for 0–3 months, other sizes are in parenthesis.

0–3 months = 14"
3–6 months = 15"
6–12 months = 16"
12–18 months = 17.5"
18–24 months = 19"

Rnd 1: With White and H hook, ch20 (ch23, ch25, ch27, ch29) 4dc in 4th ch from hook, 1sc in each of the next 15ch (18ch, 20ch, 22ch, 24ch) 4dc in last ch. Now working on opposite side of ch, 1sc in each of the next 15ch, (18ch, 20ch, 22ch, 24ch), sk beg ch3 and slst into next dc to join rnd. Continue going around using a placemarker. (38sts, 44sts, 48sts, 52sts, 56sts)

Rnd 2: Ch3, 1dc in same st as joining, 2dc in next 3dc, 1sc in next 15sc (18sc, 20sc, 22sc, 24sc), 2dc in next 4dc, 1sc in next 15sc (18sc, 20sc, 22sc, 24sc). Slst in top of ch3 to join rnd. (46sts, 52sts, 56sts, 60sts, 64sts)

Rnd 3: Ch1, (dc tog the next 2dc) x 4, 1sc in next 15sc (18sc, 20sc, 22sc, 24sc), (dc tog the next 2dc) x 4, 1sc in next 15sc (18sc, 20sc, 22sc, 24sc). Slst to join rnd. (38sts, 44sts, 48sts, 52sts, 56sts)

Rnd 4: Ch1, 1sc in same st as joining, 1sc in each st around. Do not slst to join rnd, but now work in continuous rnds. (38sc, 44sc, 48sc, 52sc, 56sc)

Rnd 5: 1sc in each sc around. (38sc, 44sc, 48sc, 52sc, 56sc)

Repeat rnd 5 until hat measures 4", (4.5", 5", 6", 6.5")

First Earflap

Row 1: 1sc in next 6sc. Turn. Leaving the rest of the row unworked for now.

Rows 2–3: Ch1, 1sc in next 8sc. Turn. (8sc)

Row 4: Ch1, sc tog the first 2sc, 1sc in next 4sc, sc tog the last 2sc. Turn. (6sc)

Row 5: Ch1, 1sc in next 6sc. Turn. (6sc)

Row 6: Ch1, sc tog the first 2sc, 1sc in next 2sc, sc tog the last 2sc. Turn. (4sc)

Row 7: Ch1, 1sc in next 4sc. Turn. (4sc)

Row 8: Ch1, (sc tog the next 2sc) x 2. Turn. (2sc)

Row 9: Ch1, 1sc in next 2sc. Do not turn. Ch1. (2sc)

Next: 1slst in each end of row down left side of earflap, 1sc in next 20sc (22sc, 24sc, 26, 28) Turn.

Second Earflap

Row 1: 1sc in next 8sc. Ch1, turn. (8sc)

Row 2: 1sc in next 8sc. Ch1, turn. (8sc)

Row 3: Sc tog the first 2sc, 1sc in next 4sc, sc tog the last 2sc. Ch1, turn. (6sc)

Row 4: 1sc in next 6sc. Ch1, turn. (6sc)

Row 5: Sc tog the first 2sc, 1sc in next 2sc, sc tog the last 2sc. Ch1, turn. (4sc)

Row 6: 1sc in next 4sc. (4sc)

Row 7: (sc tog the next 2sc) x 2. Ch1, turn. (2sc)

Row 8: 1sc in next 2sc. Do not turn. Ch1. (2sc)

Next: 1slst in each end of row down left side of earflap, 1sc in next each rem sc on last rnd.

Next: 1sc around entire hat and earflaps, and at the same time when you get to the tip of each earflap, sc, ch4, sc in tip to place braids in later.

Outside Trim

Rnd 1: Holding aqua and Green together, attach yarn to any sc, 1sc in each sc around entire hat for all sizes. Fasten off colors and weave in ends.

BRAIDS

Cut 6 strands of aqua, Green and White approx 32" long or to desired length. You will have 3 strands of each color for each braid. You are going to make two braids. Gather together your 3 strands of each color and pull through the ch4 loop in the tip of each earflap. Braid your colors together and wrap a strand around the bottom to hold all the strands together.

EYES

make 2

Rnd 1: With aqua and F hook, make a magic circle (see p. 4), work 6sc in center of loop. Pull loop tight. Work in continuous rnds. (6sc)

Rnd 2: 2sc in each sc around. (12sc)

Rnd 3: *1sc in next sc, 2sc in next sc* rep from * to * around. (18sc)

Rnd 4: *1sc in next 2sc, 2sc in next sc* rep from * to * around. (24sc)

Fasten off leaving a tail to sew with and sew on front of hat. Embroider sleeping eyes or draw on with puff paint or sew animal eyes on securely.

BEAK

Row 1: With Green and F hook, ch2, 1sc in 2nd ch from hook. Ch1, turn. (1sc)

Row 2: 2sc in next sc. Ch1, turn. (2sc)

Row 3: 2sc in next 2sc. Ch1, turn. (4sc)

You now are going to work all the way around rows 1 – 3

Rnd 1: 1sc in each end of row and in all 3 corners work 3sc. Slst to join. Fasten off leaving a tail to sew with. Sew beak onto front of hat.

Cut 1 strand of each color and tie in a knot on corners on top of hat. Trim to about an inch long.

Owl Costume stitches

(Fig 1) crotch and leg opening. (See rnd 7 on p. 77.)

(Fig 2) sc around leg opening. (See note on p. 77.)

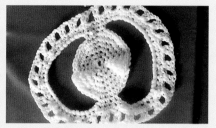

(Fig 3) crochet and foundation rnd. (See rnd 10 on p. 77.)

(Fig 4) 5dc around 1st dc post. (See rnd 11 on p. 77.)

(Fig 5) full feather. (See rnd 11 on p. 77.)

(Fig 6) arm feather. (Refers to rnds 1–8 on p. 80.)

(Fig 7) detail of finger loop on arm feather. (See rnd 8 on p. 80.)

(Fig 8) closing cluster stitches. (Refers to Bootie rnds 6–8 on p. 80.)

(Fig 9) toes formed. (Refers to Bootie rnds 6–8 on p. 80.)

(Fig 10) cluster forming toes. (Refers to Bootie rnds 6–8 on p. 80.)

Owl Mobile

Your infant won't hoot or holler when mesmerized by this charming owl mobile. Lull your little one to sleep amongst a flock of slumbering owls.

Yarn

Cascade Superwash 220 3.5oz/100g/220yds/200m/
  #4 medium weight

Colors used in pictures:

Color number 849 / Color name: Dark Aqua x 1 skein

Color number 851 / Color name: Lime x 1 skein

Color number 825 / Color name: Orange x 1 skein

Color number 815 / Color name: Black x small amount for eyes

Needle

US G6/4.00mm Susan Bates hook

Yarn Needle

Also Needed

Polyester Fiberfil x 1 bag

Mobile parts (you can look in second hand shops for the mobile parts. Or purchase one on ebay)

Gauge

15sc x 18sc rows = 4"

Glossary of Abbreviations

sc = single crochet

dc = double crochet

rnd(s) = round(s)

ch = chain(s)

slst = slip stitch

sctog2 = single crochet together next 2sc

hdc = half double crochet

FL = front loop

OWL BODY

Rnd 1: With Dark Aqua, make a magic circle (see p. 4), 6sc inside loop, pull loop tight. (6sc) Work in continuous rnds. (Fig 1 at right refers to rnds 1–10.)

Rnd 2: 2sc in each sc around. (12sc)

Rnd 3: 2sc in each sc around. (24sc)

Rnds 4–8: 1sc in each sc around. (24sc)

Rnd 9: 1sc in next sc, sctog2, 1sc in next 9sc, sctog2, 1sc in next 10sc. (22sc)

Rnd 10: 1sc in next sc, sctog2, 1sc in next 8sc, sctog2, 1sc in next 9sc. (20sc) Fasten off and weave in ends.

OWL HEAD

Rnd 1: With Green, attach yarn to any sc, 1sc in each sc around. (20sc)

Rnds 2–4: 1sc in each sc around. (20sc)

EARS

Row 1: Ch6, slst in same sc, ch8, slst in same sc, ch6, slst in next sc, now stuff owl lightly, hold top closed and work a slst in each sc across top of head to close the top, 2nd ear: ch6, slst in next sc, ch8, slst in same sc, ch6, slst in same sc. Fasten off leaving tail about 18" long. Thread yarn needle and pull tail through to middle of head. This tail can be used to tie owls to the mobile poles. (See Fig 2 at right.)

EYES

With Black and yarn needle, embroider the sleepy eyes as shown in picture. (See Fig 3 at right.)

WINGS

make 10

Rnd 1: With Orange, ch6, 1sc in 2nd ch from hook, 1hdc in next ch, 1dc in next ch, 1hdc in next ch, 3sc in next ch. Now working on opposite side of ch, 1hdc in next ch, 1dc in next ch, 1hdc in next ch. Slst to join rnd. (See Fig 4 at right refers to rnds 1–2.)

Rnd 2: Ch1, slst in same st as joining, (ch1, slst in next st) x 5, ch3, 1slst in FL of sc, slst in same sc, (ch1, slst in next st) x 5 . Slst to join rnd. Fasten off leaving a tail to sew with. Sew one wing to each side of body.

Owl Mobile stitches

(Fig 1) owl body. Referes to rnds 1–10 at left.

(Fig 2) ear row 1 – at left.

(Fig 3) embroider eyes.

(Fig 4) sew feather to side. (See Wing rnds 1–2 at left.)

Pullover Sweater

Made from washable wool, this adorable sweater will provide countless days of warmth and comfort for the little one in your life. Whether it's a brisk winter's day or a cool summer night, your bundle of joy will be cozy all the year round.

Yarn

Cascade 220 Superwash 3.5oz/100g/220yds/200m/ #4 medium weight

Colors used in pictures:

Color number 849 / Color name: Dark Aqua (main color) x 2 (2, 2, 3, 3) skeins

Color number 871 / Color name: White x 1 skein

Color number 1917 / Color name: Vinci x 1 skein

or

Color number 836 / Color name: Pink x 2 (2, 2, 3, 3) skeins

Needle

US H8/5.00mm Susan Bates hook

US F7/3.75mm Susan Bates hook

Yarn Needle

Gauge

H hook = 15sc x 17sc rows = 4"

Glossary of Abbreviations

st(s) = stitch(es)

sl st = slip stitch

rnd(s) =round(s)

sk = skip

BL = Back loop(s)

yo = yarn over

rem = remaining

ch = chain

sc = single crochet

hdc = half double crochet

texture combo = (1sc, 1hdc) in same sc

Finished Sizes

0–3 months approx 17" chest circumference

0–3 months shoulder to bottom of sweater approx 9"

3–6 months approx 18" chest circumference

3–6 months shoulder to to bottom of sweater approx 10"

6–12 months approx 19" chest circumference

6–12 months shoulder to bottom of sweater approx 11"

12–18 months approx 20" chest circumference

12–18 months shoulder to bottom of sweater approx 13"

18–24 months approx 22" chest circumference

18–24 months shoulder to bottom of sweater approx 14"

Instructions are written 0–3, other sizes are in parenthesis

YOKE

Work all sizes to row 6.

Rnd 1: With H hook and Dark Aqua, ch48 (ch52, ch56, ch64, ch68), slst in 1st ch to form a circle, making sure not to twist ch. Ch1, 1sc in same st as joining, 1sc in each rem ch. Slst to join. (48sc, 52sc, 56sc, 64sc, 68sc). (See Fig 1 opposite.)

Rnd 2: Ch1, 1sc in same st as joining, 1sc in next 5sc (6sc, 7sc, 8sc, 9sc), 2sc in next sc, *1sc in next 10sc (10sc, 10sc, 12sc, 12sc), 2sc in next sc, 1sc in next 12sc (14sc, 16sc, 18sc, 20sc), 2sc in next sc, 1sc in next 10sc (10sc, 10sc, 12sc, 12sc), 2sc in next sc, 1sc in next 6sc (7sc, 8sc, 9sc, 10sc). Slst to join. (52sc, 56sc, 60sc, 68sc, 72sc) Fasten off.

Rnd 3: With White, attach yarn to where you fastened off, ch1, 1sc in same st as joining, 1sc in next 6sc (7sc, 8sc, 9sc, 10sc), 2sc in next sc, 1sc in next 11sc (11sc, 11sc, 13sc, 13sc), 2sc in next sc, 1sc in next 13sc (15sc, 17sc, 19sc, 21sc) 2sc in next sc, 1sc in next 11sc (11sc, 11sc, 13sc, 13sc) 2sc in next sc, 1sc in next 6sc (7sc, 8sc, 9sc, 10sc). Slst to join. (56sc, 60sc, 64sc, 72sc, 76sc). (See Fig 2 opposite.)

Rnd 4: Ch1, 1sc in same st as joining, 1sc in next 7sc (8sc, 9sc, 10sc, 11sc), 2sc in next sc, 1sc in next 12sc (12sc, 12sc, 14sc, 14sc), 2sc in next sc, 1sc in next 14sc (16sc, 18sc, 20sc, 22sc), 2sc in next sc, 1sc in next 12sc, (12sc, 12sc, 14sc, 14sc), 2sc in next sc, 1sc in next 6sc (7sc, 8sc, 9 sc, 10sc). Slst to join. (60sc, 64sc, 68sc, 76sc, 80sc) Fasten off.

Rnd 5: With Vinci, attach yarn to where you fastened off, ch1, 1sc in same st as joining, 1sc in next 8sc (9sc, 10sc, 11sc, 12sc), 2sc in next sc, 1sc in next 13sc (13sc, 13sc, 15sc, 15sc), 2sc in next sc, 1sc in next 15sc (17sc, 19sc, 21sc, 23sc), 2sc in next sc, 1sc in next 13sc (13sc, 13sc, 15sc, 15sc), 2sc in next sc, 1sc in next 6sc (7sc, 8sc, 9sc, 10sc). Slst to join. (64sc, 68sc, 72sc, 80sc, 84sc)

Rnd 6: Ch1, 1sc in same st as joining, 1sc in next 9sc (10sc, 11sc, 12sc, 13sc), 2sc in next sc, 1sc in next 14sc (14sc, 14sc, 16sc, 16sc), 2sc in next sc, 1sc in next 16sc (18sc, 20sc, 22sc, 24sc), 2sc in next sc, 1sc in next 14sc (14sc, 14sc, 16sc, 16sc), 2sc in next sc, 1sc in next 6sc (7sc, 8sc, 9sc, 10sc). Slst to join. (68sc, 72sc, 76sc, 84sc, 88sc) Fasten off.

Rnd 7: With Dark Aqua, ch1, 1sc in same st as joining, 1sc in next 10sc (11sc, 12sc, 13sc, 14sc), 2sc in next sc, 1sc in next 15sc (15sc, 15sc, 17sc, 17sc), 2sc in next sc, 1sc in next 17sc (19sc, 21sc, 23sc, 25sc), 2sc in next sc, 1sc in next 15sc, (15sc, 15sc, 17sc, 17sc), 2sc in next sc, 1sc in next 6sc (7sc, 8sc, 9sc, 10sc). Slst to join. (72sc, 76sc, 80sc, 88sc, 92sc)

Rnd 8: Ch1, 1sc in same st as joining, 1sc in next 11sc (12sc, 13sc, 14sc, 15sc), 2sc in next sc, 1sc in next 16sc (16sc, 16sc, 18sc, 18sc), 2sc in next sc, 1sc in next 18sc (20sc, 22sc, 24sc, 26sc), 2sc in next sc, 1sc in next 16sc, (16sc, 16sc, 18sc, 18sc), 2sc in next sc, 1sc in next 6sc (7sc, 8sc, 9sc, 10sc). Slst to join. (76sc, 80sc, 84sc, 92sc, 96sc) fasten off.

Rnd 9: Attach White, ch1, 1sc in same st as joining, 1sc in next 12sc (13sc, 14sc, 15sc, 16sc), 2sc in next sc, 1sc in next 17sc (17sc, 17sc, 19sc, 19sc), 2sc in next sc, 1sc in next 19sc (21sc, 23sc, 25sc, 27sc), 2sc in next sc, 1sc in next 17sc (17sc, 17sc, 19sc, 19sc), 2sc in next sc, 1sc in next 6sc (7sc, 8sc, 9sc, 10sc). Slst to join. (80sc, 84sc, 88sc, 96sc, 100sc)

Rnd 10: Ch1, 1sc in same st as joining, 1sc in next 13sc (14sc, 15sc, 16sc, 17sc), 2sc in next sc, 1sc in next 18sc (18sc, 18sc, 20sc, 20sc), 2sc in next sc, 1sc in next 20sc (22sc, 24sc, 26sc, 28sc), 2sc in next sc, 1sc in next 18sc, (18sc, 18sc, 20sc, 20sc), 2sc in next sc, 1sc in next 6sc (7sc, 8sc, 9sc, 10sc). Slst to join. (84sc, 88sc, 92sc, 100sc, 104sc) Fasten off.

Stop after here to complete 0–3 months yoke. Continue on to armhold openings for 0–3 months. (See Fig 3 opposite.)

Complete rnds 11–12 for 3–6 months yoke
Complete rnds 11–14 for 6–12 months yoke
Complete rnds 11–16 for 12–18 months yoke
Complete rnds 11–18 for 18–24 months yoke

3–6 months Yoke

Rnd 11: Attach Vinci, ch1, 1sc in same st as joining, 1sc in next 15sc (16sc, 17sc, 18sc), 2sc in next sc, 1sc in next 19sc (19sc, 21sc, 21sc), 2sc in next sc, 1sc in next 23sc (25sc, 27sc, 29sc), 2sc in next sc, 1sc in next 19sc (19sc, 21sc, 21sc), 2sc in next sc, 1sc in next 7sc (7sc, 9sc, 10sc). Slst to join. (92sc, 96sc, 104sc, 108sc)

Rnd 12: Ch1, 1sc in same st as joining, 1sc in next 16sc (17sc, 18sc, 19sc), 2sc in next sc, 1sc in next 20sc (20sc, 22sc, 22sc), 2sc in next sc, 1sc in next 24sc (26sc, 28sc, 30sc), 2sc in next sc, 1sc in next 20sc (20sc, 22sc, 22sc), 2sc in next sc, 1sc in next 7sc (8sc, 9sc, 10sc). Slst to join. (96sc, 100sc, 108sc, 112sc) Fasten off.

Stop after here to complete 3–6 months yoke. Continue on to armhold openings for 3–6 months.

6–12 months Yoke

Rnd 13: Attach Dark Aqua21, Ch1, 1sc in same st as joining, 1sc in next 18sc, (19sc, 20sc), 2sc in next sc, 1sc in next 21sc, (23sc, 23sc), 2sc in next sc, 1sc in next 27sc, (29sc, 31sc), 2sc in next sc,

Pullover Sweater stitches

(Fig 1) slst to form circle for neck. (See Yoke rnd 1 opposite.)

(Fig 2) add first white row. (See Yoke rnd 3 opposite.)

(Fig 3) yoke. (See opposite – refers to to rnds 10, 11–12, 11–14, 11–16, 11–24.)

(Fig 4) rnd 1 of ribbing rows. (See p. 93.)

(Fig 5) working in the BL. (See row 2 p. 93.)

(Fig 6) slst in next 2sc. (See row 3 p. 93.)

1sc in next 21sc, (23sc, 23sc), 2sc in next sc, 1sc in next 8sc, (9sc, 10sc). Slst to join. (104sc, 112sc, 116sc)

Rnd 14: Ch1, 1sc in same st as joining, 1sc in next 19sc (20sc, 21sc), 2sc in next sc, 1sc in next 22sc, (24sc, 24sc), 2sc in next sc, 1sc in next 28sc, (30sc, 32sc), 2sc in next sc, 1sc in next 22sc, (24sc, 24sc), 2sc in next sc, 1sc in next 8sc, (9sc, 10sc). Slst to join. (108sc, (116sc, 120sc) Do not fasten off.

Stop after here to complete 6–12 month yoke. Continue onto armhold openings for 6–12 months.

12–18 months Yoke
Rnd 15: Attach White, ch1, 1sc in same st as joining, 1sc in next 21sc, (22sc), 2sc in next sc, 1sc in next 25sc (25sc), 2sc in next sc, 1sc in next 31sc, (33sc), 2sc in next sc, 1sc in next 21sc 25sc, (25sc), 2sc in next sc, 1sc in next 9sc, (10sc). Slst to join. (120sc, 124sc)

Rnd 16: Ch1, 1sc in same st as joining, 1sc in next 22sc, (23sc), 2sc in next sc, 1sc in next 26sc, (26sc), 2sc in next sc, 1sc in next 32sc, (34sc), 2sc in next sc, 1sc in next 26sc, (26sc), 2sc in next sc, 1sc in next 9sc, (10sc). Slst to join. (124sc, 128sc) Fasten off.

Stop after here to complete 12–18 month yoke. Continue on to armhold openings for 12–18 months.

18–24 months Yoke
Rnd 17: Attach Vinci, ch1, 1sc in same st as joining, 1sc in next 24sc, 2sc in next sc, 1sc in next 27sc, 2sc in next sc, 1sc in next 35sc, 2sc in next sc, 1sc in next 27sc, 2sc in next sc, 1sc in next 10sc. Slst to join. (132sc)

Rnd 18: Ch1, 1sc in same st as joining, 1sc in next 25sc, 2sc in next sc, 1sc in next 28sc, 2sc in next sc, 1sc in next 36sc, 2sc in next sc, 1sc in next 28sc, 2sc in next sc, 1sc in next 10sc. Slst to join. (136sc) Fasten off. Continue on to armhole openings.

Forming Armhold Openings
Start all sizes with MC.

Rnd 1: Ch1, 1sc in same st as joining, 1sc in next 14sc (17sc, 20sc, 23sc, 26sc) sk next 20sc (23sc, 24sc, 28sc, 30sc) 1sc in next 22sc (26sc, 30sc, 34sc, 38sc) sk next 20sc (23sc, 24sc, 28sc, 30sc) 1sc in next 7sc (8sc, 9sc, 10sc, 11sc). Slst to join. (44sc, 52sc 60sc, 68sc, 76sc)

BODY

Rnd 1: Ch1, 1sc in same st as joining, 1sc in next 2sc, 2sc in next sc, *1sc in next 3sc, 2sc in next sc*, rep from * to * around. Slst to join rnd. (55sc, 65sc, 75sc, 85sc, 95sc)

Rnd 2: Ch1, 2sc in same st as joining, 1sc in each sc around. Work in continuous spiral fashion. (56sc, 66sc, 76sc, 86sc, 96sc)

Rnd 3: (1sc, 1hdc) in next sc, sk next sc *(1sc, 1hdc) in next sc, sk next sc*, rep from * to * around. Work in a continuous spiral fashion. (56sts, 66sts, 76sts, 86sts, 96sts)

Rnd 4: (1sc, 1hdc) in next sc, sk next hdc, *(1sc, 1hdc) in next sc, sk next hdc* rep from * to * around. Continue to work in a spiral fashion. (56sts, 66sc, 76sts, 86sts, 96sts)

Repeat rnd 4 until sweaters measures

0–3 months: shoulder to bottom of sweater = 9"
3–6 months: shoulder to bottom of sweater = 10"
6–12 months: shoulder to bottom of sweater = 11"
12–18 months: shoulder to bottom of sweater = 13"
18–24 months: shoulder to bottom of sweater = 14"

Ribbing on Bottom of Sweater

Rnd 1: With Vinci, and with G hook, attach yarn to any st on bottom of sweater, ch1, 1sc in same st as joining, 1sc in each st around. Slst to join. (See Fig 4 on p. 91.)

You now are going to work in rows to make the ribs.

Row 1: Ch 5, 1sc in 2nd ch from hook, 1sc in next 3ch, 1slst in next 2sc on rnd 1 on bottom of sweater. Turn. (4sc)

Row 2: Ch1, sk next 2slsts, 1sc in the BL of next 4sc. Turn. (4sc). (See Fig 5 on p. 91.)

Row 3: Ch1, 1sc in BL of next 4sc, 1slst in next 2sc on rnd 1 of bottom of sweater. Turn. (4sc) (See Fig 6 on p. 91.)

Repeat rows 2 and 3 alternately around end of sweater. Fasten off leaving a tail to sew with. Sew 1st row to last row to close ribbing.

SLEEVES

Rnd 1: With H hook and Dark Aqua, attach yarn to bottom of armhole opening, 1sc in same st as joining, work (26sc, 28sc, 30sc, 32sc, 34sc) around opening. Slst to join. (26sc, 28sc, 30sc, 32sc, 34sc)

Rnd 2: Ch1, (1sc, 1hdc) in same st as joining, sk next sc *(1sc, 1hdc) in next sc, sk next sc*, rep from * to * around. Work in a continuous spiral fashion. (26sts, 28sts, 30sts, 32sts, 34sts)

Rnds 3: (1sc, 1hdc) in next sc, sk next hdc, *(1sc, 1hdc) in next sc, sk next hdc* rep from * to * around. (26sts, 28sts, 30sts, 32sts, 34sts)

Work in a continuous spiral fashion.

Repeat rnd 3 until sleeve measures from underarm to end of sleeve.

0–3 months = 5"
3–6 months = 5.5"
6–12 months = 6"
12–18 months = 6.5"
18–24 months = 7"

Note: you will add approx another inch after you make the ribbings.

Ribbing for Neck and Arms

Rnd 1: With Vinci, and with G hook, attach yarn to any st, ch1, 1sc in same st as joining, 1sc in each st around. Slst to join.

You now are going to work in rows to make the ribs.

Row 1: Ch 4, 1sc in 2nd ch from hook, 1sc in next 2ch, 1slst in next 2sc. Turn. (3sc)

Row 2: Ch1, sk next 2slsts, 1sc in the BL of next 3sc. Turn. (3sc)

Row 3: Ch1, 1sc in BL of next 3sc, 1slst in next 2sc. Turn. (3sc)

Repeat rows 2 and 3 alternately around. Fasten off leaving a tail to sew with.

Sew 1st row to last row.

Romper Set

Blending the beauty of today with the history of yesteryear, this adorable romper is reminiscent of a time long ago. Whether at the beach or enjoying a warm summer day, this cool and comfortable cotton set is perfect for the active little girl in your life.

Yarn

Cascade Ultra Pima Cotton 1.75oz/50g/136.7yds/125m/ #2 fine weight cotton

Colors used in pictures:

Main Color (MC): Color number 3753 / Color name: White Peach x 3 (3, 4, 5, 5) hanks

Trim Color: Roses color: Color number 3750 / Color name: Tangerine x 1 hank

Color number 3746 / Color name: Chartreuse x 1 hank for leaves and ribbon

Or desired colors

Buttons

3 x ½" buttons

Needle

US D3/3.25MM Susan Bates Hook

US E4/3.50MM Susan Bates Hook

US F5/3.75MM Susan Bates Hook

Tapestry Needle

Gauge

Gauge: E hook = 10sc x 10sc rows = 2"

F hook = 9sc x 9sc rows = 2"

Glossary of Abbreviations

st(s) = stitch(es)

beg = beginning

rem = remaining

sk = skip

BL = back loop

FL = front loop

chsp = chain

ch = chain

sc = single crochet

dc = double crochet

sp = space

rep from * to * = repeat between the stars

slst = slip stitch

rnd(s) = round(s)

trc = treble crochet

hdc = half double crochet

fpdc = front post double crochet

vshell = (2dc, ch1, 2dc) all in next sc or ch1sp

fpdc = front post double crochet = yo and draw up a loop around post, (yo and draw through 2 loops on hook) twice.

Finished Sizes

0–3 approx 17" chest – shoulder to crotch approx 12"

3–6 approx 18" chest – shoulder to crotch approx 13"

6–12 approx 19" chest – shoulder to crotch approx 14"

12–18 approx 20" chest – shoulder to crotch approx 16"

18–24 approx 22" chest – shoulder to crotch approx 17"

Instructions are written 0–3, other sizes are in parenthesis

BODICE

(Note: See Romper Set stitches p. 98)

Work all sizes to row 7.

Row 1: With F hook and desired MC, ch36 (ch39, ch42, ch45, ch48), 1sc in 2nd ch from hook, 1sc in each rem ch. Turn. (35sc, 38sc, 41sc, 44sc, 47sc). (See Fig 1 p. 98.)

Row 2: Ch3, 1dc in next 4sc (5sc, 5sc, 6sc, 6sc), vshell, 1dc in next 5sc (5sc, 6sc, 6sc, 7sc,), vshell, 1dc in next 11sc (12sc, 13sc, 14sc, 15sc), vshell, 1dc in next 5sc (5sc, 6sc, 6sc, 7sc), vshell, 1dc in next 5sc (6sc, 6sc, 7sc, 7sc). Turn. (47dc, 50dc, 53dc, 56dc, 59dc)

Row 3: Ch3, 1dc in next 6dc (7dc, 7dc, 8dc, 8dc), vshell, 1dc in next 9dc (9dc, 10dc, 10dc, 11dc), vshell, 1dc in next 15dc (16dc, 17dc, 18dc, 19dc), vshell, 1dc in next 9dc (9dc, 10dc, 10dc, 11dc), vshell, 1dc in next 7dc (8dc, 8dc, 9dc, 9dc). Turn. (63dc, 66dc, 69dc, 72dc, 75dc)

Row 4: Ch3, 1dc in next 8dc, (9dc, 9dc, 10dc, 10dc), vshell, 1dc in next 13dc (13dc, 14dc, 14dc, 15dc), vshell, 1dc in next 19dc (20dc, 21dc, 22dc, 23dc), vshell, 1dc in next 13dc (13dc, 14dc, 14dc, 15dc), vshell, 1dc in next 9dc (10dc, 10dc, 11dc, 11dc). Turn. (79dc, 82dc, 85dc, 88dc, 91dc)

Row 5: Ch3, 1dc in next 10dc (11dc, 11dc, 12dc, 12dc), vshell, 1dc in next 17dc, (17dc, 18dc, 18dc, 19dc), vshell, 1dc in next 23dc (24dc, 25dc, 26dc, 27dc), vshell, 1dc in next 17dc (17dc, 18dc, 18dc, 19dc), vshell, 1dc in next 11dc (12dc, 12dc, 13dc, 13dc). Turn. (95dc, 98dc, 101dc, 104dc, 107dc)

Row 6: Ch3, 1dc in next 12dc (13dc, 13dc, 14dc, 14dc), vshell, 1dc in next 21dc (21dc, 22dc, 22dc, 23dc), vshell, 1dc in next 27dc (28dc, 29dc, 30dc, 31dc), vshell, 1dc in next 21dc (21dc, 22dc, 22dc, 23dc), vshell, 1dc in next 13dc (14dc, 14dc, 15dc, 15dc). Turn. (111dc, 114dc, 117dc, 120dc, 123dc)

Row 7: Ch3, 1dc in next 14dc (15dc, 15dc, 16dc, 16dc), vshell, 1dc in next 25dc (25dc, 26dc, 26dc, 27dc), vshell, 1dc in next 31dc (32dc, 33dc, 34dc, 35dc), vshell, 1dc in next 25dc (25dc, 26dc, 26dc, 27dc), vshell, 1dc in next 15dc (16dc, 16dc, 17dc, 17dc). Turn. (127dc, 130 dc, 133dc, 136dc, 139dc)

Continue on to armhole opening except for 18–24 months.

Size 18–24 months only Bodice:

Row 8: Ch3, 1dc in next 18dc, vshell, 1dc in next 31dc, vshell, 1dc in next 39dc, vshell, 1dc in next 31dc, vshell, 1dc in next 19dc. Turn. (155dc) Continue on to form armhole openings.

Forming Armhole Openings

Row 1: Ch3, 1dc in next 16dc (17dc, 17dc, 18dc, 20dc), 1dc in next ch1sp, sk next 29dc (29dc, 30dc, 30dc, 35dc), 1dc in next ch1sp, 1dc in next 35dc (36dc, 37dc, 38dc, 43dc), 1dc in next ch1sp, sk next 29dc (29dc, 30dc, 30dc, 35dc), 1dc in next ch1sp, 1dc in next 17dc (18dc, 18dc, 19dc, 21dc). (73dc, 76dc, 77dc, 80dc, 89dc). (See Figs 2 and 3 on p. 98.)

BUTTONBANDS

Row 1: Working in ends of rows, work sc up right button hole band to neck edge. Turn. (12sc, 12sc, 12sc, 17sc, 17sc)

Row 2: Ch1, 1sc in next sc, ch2, sk next sc, 1sc in next 3sc (3sc, 3sc, 5sc, 5sc) ch2, sk next sc, 1sc in next 3sc (3sc, 3sc, 4sc, 4sc), ch2, sk next sc, 1sc in next 2sc (2sc, 2sc, 4sc, 4sc). Turn.

Row 3: Ch1, 1sc in each sc and 1sc in each ch2sp across. (12sc, 12sc, 12sc, 17sc, 17sc) Continue on to neck edge.

Neck Edge

Row 1: 1sc in each st across neck edge to left front.

Left Band

Row 1: Work 12sc (12sc, 12sc, 17sc, 17sc) down left front. Turn. (12sc, 12sc, 12sc, 17sc, 17sc)

Rows 2–3: Ch1, 1sc in each sc across. Turn. (12sc, 12sc, 12sc, 17sc, 17sc)

PANTS

Rnd 1: Next overlap button hole band over left band, working through both thicknesses, *1sc in next 2sts, 2sc in next st* rep from * to * around, adjusting your stitches to that you work out the numbers to be 96sc (104sc, 104sc, 112sc, 112sc). Slst to join. (96sc, 104sc, 104sc, 112sc, 112sc). (See Fig 4 p. 98.)

Rnd 2: Ch1, 1sc in BL of same st as joining, 1sc in BL of each sc around. Slst to join rnd. (96sc, 104sc, 104sc, 112sc, 112sc)

Rnd 3: Ch3, sk next sc, vshell in next sc, sk next sc, *1dc in next sc, sk next sc, vshell in next sc, sk next sc* rep from * to * around ending with sk last 2sc. Slst to top of ch3 to join rnd. (24vshells, 26vshells, 26vshells, 28vshells, 28vshells)

Rnd 4: Ch3, vshell in middle of vshell, *fpdc around next dc, vshell in middle of vshell* rep from * to * around. Slst to top of ch3 to join rnd.

Romper Set stitches

(Fig 1) yoke. (See Bodice, Row 1 p. 96.)

(Fig 2) armhole. (See Forming Armhole Opening. Row 1 p. 96.)

(Fig 3) making sleeve. (See Sleeves, opposite, Rnd 1.)

(Fig 4) pant legs. (See Pants, Rnd 1 p. 96.)

(Fig 5) starting trim on sleeves or legs. (See opposite, Sleeve Cuff Trims and Leg Cuff Trims, Rnd 1.)

(Fig 6) trim on sleeves or legs.

(Fig 7) picot on sleeves or legs. (See opposite, Sleeve Cuff Trims and Leg Cuff Trims, Rnd 3.)

(Fig 8) start of roses. (See Roses, opposite and p. 100.)

(Fig 9) put 9 sc through layers to form a rose.

Rnds 5–23 (5–26, 5–29, 5–32, 5–35): Ch3, vshell in middle of vshell, *fpdc around next fpdc, vshell in middle of vshell* rep from * to * around. Slst to top of ch3 to join rnd. Or until 12", (13", 14", 16", 17") long from top of shoulder to last rnd.

LEGS

Rnd 1: Now fold romper flat and find the center where you will form the crotch. Working through both thicknesses, ch1, 1sc through both side of romper to form a crotch. Ch3, vshell in middle of vshell, *fpdc around next fpdc, vshell in middle of vshell* rep from * to * around. Slst to top of ch3 to join first leg.

Rnds 2–3: Ch3, vshell in middle of vshell, *fpdc around next fpdc, vshell in middle of vshell* rep from * to * around. Slst to top of ch3 to join rnd.

Note: you will have (12vshells, 13vshells, 13vshells, 14vshells, 14vshells) on each leg.

Leg Cuff Trims

Rnd 1: With desired trim color, attach yarn to any FL on rnd 5, 1sc in same st as joining, 1sc in each FL around. Slst to join. (See Fig 5.)

Rnd 2: 1sc in same st as joining, ch3, sk next 2sc, *1sc in next sc, ch3, sk next 2sc* rep from * to * around. Slst to join.

Rnd 3: 1sc in same st as joining, 2sc in next ch loop, ch3, 1slst in top of 3rd sc, 2sc in same ch loop, *1slst in next sc, 3sc in next ch loop, ch3, 1slst in top of 3rd sc, 2sc in same ch loop* rep from * to * around. Slst to join. Fasten off, leaving a tail to sew with. If desired tack down rnd 3 to sleeve cuff. (See Fig 7.)

Cuff

Rnd 1: Ch1, 1sc in same st as joining, 1sc in next dc, sk next dc, 1sc in next ch1sp, sk next dc, *1sc in next dc, sk next fpdc, 1sc in next dc, sk next dc, 1sc in next ch1sp, sk next dc* rep from * to * around. Slst to join.

Rnd 2: Ch1, 1sc in BL of same st as joining, 1sc in BL of next sc, *sc tog in the BL of the next 2sc, 1sc in the BL of the next 2sc* rep from * to * around. Slst to join.

Rnds 3–7: Ch1, 1sc in same st as joining, 1sc in each sc around. Slst to join. End of last rnd fasten off and weave in ends.

Second leg cuff: attach yarn to any sc on second leg, repeat rnds 1–7.

SLEEVES

make 2

Rnd 1: With desired MC and F hook, attach yarn to underarm opening, ch3, 1dc in next 6sts (6sts, 9sts, 9sts, 9sts), 2dc in next 13sts (13sts, 16sts, 16sts, 20sts), 1dc in next 7sts (7sts, 10sts, 10sts, 10sts). Slst to join rnd. (40dc, 40dc, 52dc, 52dc, 60dc). (See Fig 3.)

Rnds 2–3: Ch3, 1dc in each dc around. Slst to join rnd. (40dc, 40dc, 52dc, 52dc, 60dc)

Rnd 4: Ch1, *sc tog the next 2dc* rep from * to * around. Slst to join. (20sc, 20sc, 26sc, 26sc, 30sc)

Rnd 5: Ch1, 1sc in BL of same st as joining, 1sc in BL of each sc around. Slst to join. (20sc, 20sc, 26sc, 26sc, 30sc)

Rnds 6–9: Ch1, 1sc in same st as joining, 1sc in each sc around. Slst to join. (20sc, 20sc, 26sc, 26sc, 30sc) end of rnd 9 fasten off and weave in ends. (See Fig 6 opposite).

Sleeve Cuff Trims

Rnd 1: With desired trim color, attach yarn to any FL on rnd 5, 1sc in same st as joining, 1sc in each FL around. slst to join. (20sc, 20sc, 26sc, 26sc, 30sc)

Rnd 2: 1sc in same st as joining, ch3, sk next sc, *1sc in next sc, ch3, sk next sc* rep from * to * around. Slst to join.

Rnd 3: 1sc in same st as joining, 2sc in next ch loop, ch3, 1slst in top of 3rd sc, 2sc in same ch loop, *1slst in next sc, 3sc in next ch loop, ch3, 1slst in top of 3rd sc, 2sc in same ch loop* rep from * to * around. Slst to join. Fasten off leaving a tail to sew with. If desired tack down rnd 3 to sleeve cuff. (See Fig 7 opposite).

Neck Trim

Row 1: Attach desired trim color to first sc on neck edge, 1sc in same st as joining, 1sc in each sc across neck edge and across ends of rows on buttonbands. Turn.

Row 2: Ch1, 1sc in the BL of each sc across. Turn

Row 3: Ch1, 1sc in first sc, *ch3, sk next 2sc, 1sc in next sc* rep from * to * across. Turn.

Row 4: 1slst in first sc, *3sc in next chloop, ch3, 1slst in top of last sc, 2sc in same ch loop, 1slst in next sc* rep from * to * across. Slst in last sc. Fasten off leaving a tail to sew with. Tack row 4 down if desired.

ROSES

First rose: With F hook and with desired rose color, attach yarn to FL from rnd 1 on back of pants, ch10, 2sc in 2nd ch from hook, 2sc in next 2ch, 2hdc in next 3ch, 2dc in next 3ch. Roll stitches into a rose shape and crochet a sc to hold rose together, as shown in the picture. (See Figs 8 and 9, p. 98.)

Second rose: Skip next 4FL, 1sc in next FL, ch10, 2sc in 2nd ch from hook, 2sc in next 2ch, 2hdc in next 3ch, 2dc in next 3ch. Roll stitches into a rose shape and crochet a sc to hold rose together, as shown in the picture. Continue working roses like second rose until you are all the way around.

SUNHAT
Work rnds 1–7 for all sizes.

Rnd 1: With MC and E hook, ch2, 6sc in 2nd ch from hook. (6sc) Work in continuous rnds.

Rnd 2: 2sc in each sc around. (12sc)

Rnd 3: *1sc in next sc, 2sc in next sc* rep from * to* around. (18sc)

Rnd 4: *1sc in next 2sc, 2sc in next sc* rep from * to* around. (24sc)

Rnd 5: *1sc in next 3sc, 2sc in next sc* rep from * to* around. (30sc)

Rnd 6: *1sc in next 4sc, 2sc in next sc* rep from * to* around. (36sc)

Rnd 7: *1sc in next 5sc, 2sc in next sc* rep from * to* around. (42sc)

0–3 months
Rnd 8: 1sc in BL of each sc around. (42sc)

Rnd 9: Slst in next sc, ch3, (1dc, ch1, 2dc) in same st, *sk next sc, 1dc in next sc, sk next sc, (2dc, ch1, 2dc) in next sc* rep from * to * around to last 5sc, sk next 2sc, 1dc in next sc, sk next 2sc. Slst to top of ch3 to join. (10 vshells,)

Rnd 10: Slst in next ch1sp, beg vshell, 1fpdc around next dc, *vshell in next ch1sp, 1fpdc around next dc* rep from * to * around. Slst to top of ch3 to join rnd. (10vshells)

Rnds 11–15: Slst in next ch1sp, beg vshell, 1fpdc around next fpdc, *vshell in next ch1sp, 1fpdc around next fpdc* rep from * to * around. Slst to top of ch3 to join rnd. (10vshells)

Rnd 16: Ch1, 1sc in same st as joining, *sk next dc, 1sc in chsp, sk next dc, 1sc in next dc, 1sc in next fpdc, 1sc in next dc* rep from * to * around. Slst to join rnd. (40sc)

Change to D hook

Rnd 17: With D hook, ch1, 1sc in BL of same st as joining*2sc in BL of next sc, 1sc in BL of next sc* rep from * to * around. Slst to join rnd.

Rnd 18: Ch3, sk next 2sc, vshell in next sc, sk next 2sc, 1dc in next sc, sk next 2sc, *vshell in next sc, sk next 2sc, 1dc in next sc, sk next 2sc* rep from * to * around. Slst to 3rd ch to join rnd.

Rnd 19: ch1, 1sc in same st as joining, ch1, *6dc in vshell, ch1, 1sc in next dc, ch1* rep from * to * around. Slst to join rnd. Fasten off and weave in ends.

Follow same instructions as for roses around waist of romper working on rnd 8 of hat.

3–6 months
Rnd 8: *1sc in next 6sc, 2sc in next sc* rep from * to * around. (48sc)

Rnd 9: 1sc in BL of each sc around. (48sc)

Rnd 10: Slst in next sc, ch3, (1dc, ch1, 2dc) in same st, *sk next sc, 1dc in next sc, sk next sc, (2dc, ch1, 2dc) in next sc* rep from * to * around to last 2sc, sk next 2sc. Slst to top of ch3 to join. (12vshells)

Rnd 11: Slst in next ch1sp, beg vshell, 1fpdc around next dc, *vshell in next ch1sp, 1fpdc around next dc* rep from * to * around. Slst to top of ch3 to join rnd. (12 vshells)

Rnds 12–17: Slst in next ch1sp, beg vshell, 1fpdc around next fpdc, *vshell in next ch1sp, 1fpdc around next fpdc* rep from * to * around. Slst to top of ch3 to join rnd. (12vshells)

Rnd 18: Ch1, 1sc in same st as joining, *sk next dc, 1sc in chsp, sk next dc, 1sc in next dc, 1sc in next fpdc, 1sc in next dc* rep from * to * around. Slst to join rnd. (48sc)

Change to D hook

Rnd 19: With D hook, ch1, 1sc in BL of same st as joining *2sc in BL of next sc, 1sc in BL pf next sc* rep from * to* around. Slst to join rnd.

Rnd 20: Ch3, sk next 2sc, vshell in next sc, sk next 2sc, 1dc in next sc, sk next 2sc, *vshell in next sc, sk next 2sc, 1dc in next sc, sk next 2sc* rep from * to * around. Slst to 3rd ch to join rnd.

Rnd 21: ch1, 1sc in same st as joining, ch1, *6dc in vshell, ch1, 1sc in next dc, ch1* rep from * to * around. Slst to join rnd. Fasten off and weave in ends.

Follow same instructions as for roses around waist of romper working on rnd 9 of hat.

6–12 months

Rnd 8: *1sc in next 6sc, 2sc in next sc* rep from * to* around. (48sc)

Rnd 9: *1sc in next 7sc, 2sc in next sc* rep from * to* around. (54sc)

Rnd 10: 1sc in BL of each sc around. (54sc)

Rnd 11: Slst in next sc, ch3, (1dc, ch1, 2dc) in same st, sk next sc, 1dc in next sc, sk next sc* (2dc, ch1, 2dc) in next sc, sk next 2sc, 1dc in next sc, sk next sc* rep from * to * around. . Slst to join rnd. (13 vshells,)

Rnd 12: Slst in next ch1sp, beg vshell, sk 2dc of vshell, 1fpdc around next dc, *vshell in next ch1sp, sk 2dc o f vshell, 1fpdc around next dc* rep from * to * around. Slst to join rnd. (13vshells)

Rnds 13–18: Slst in next ch1sp, beg vshell, 1fpdc around next fpdc, *vshell in next ch1sp, 1fpdc around next fpdc* rep from * to * around. Slst to join rnd. (13vshells)

Rnd 19: Ch1, 1sc in same st as joining, *sk next dc, 1sc in chsp, sk next dc, 1sc in next dc, 1sc in next fpdc, 1sc in next dc* rep from * to * around. Slst to join rnd. (52sc)

Change to D hook

Rnd 20: With D hook, ch1, 1sc in BL of same st as joining, *2sc in BL of next sc, 1sc in BL of next sc* rep from * to* around. Slst to join rnd.

Rnd 21: Ch3, sk next sc, vshell in next sc, sk next sc, 1dc in next sc, sk next sc, vshell in next sc, sk next sc *1dc in next sc, sk next sc, vshell in next sc, sk next sc* rep from * to * to last 2sc. Slst to join rnd.

Rnd 22: Ch1, 1sc in same st as joining, ch1, *6dc in vshell, ch1, 1sc in next dc, ch1* rep from * to * around. Slst to join rnd. Fasten off and weave in ends.

Follow same instructions as for roses around waist of romper, working on rnd 10 of hat.

12–18 months

Rnd 8: *1sc in next 6sc, 2sc in next sc* rep from * to * around. (48sc)

Rnd 9: *1sc in next 7sc, 2sc in next sc* rep from * to * around. (54sc)

Rnd 10: *1sc in next 8sc, 2sc in next sc* rep from * to * around. (60sc)

Rnd 11: 1sc in BL of each sc around. (60sc)

Rnd 12: Slst in next sc, ch3, (1dc, ch1, 2dc) in same st, *sk next sc, 1dc in next sc, sk next sc, (2dc, ch1, 2dc) in next sc* rep from * to* around. Slst to top of ch3 to join. (15 vshells,)

Rnd 13: Slst in next ch1sp, beg vshell, 1fpdc around next dc, *vshell in next ch1sp, 1fpdc around next dc* rep from * to * around. Slst to top of ch3 to join rnd. (15vshells)

Rnds 14–20: Slst in next ch1sp, beg vshell, 1fpdc around next fpdc, *vshell in next ch1sp, 1fpdc around next fpdc* rep from * to * around. Slst to top of ch3 to join rnd. (15vshells)

Rnd 21: Ch1, 1sc in same st as joining, *sk next dc, 1sc in chsp, sk next dc, 1sc in next dc, 1sc in next fpdc, 1sc in next dc* rep from * to * around. Slst to join rnd. (60sc)

Change to D hook

Rnd 22: With D hook, ch1, 1sc in BL of same st as joining, *2sc in BL of next sc, 1sc in BL of next sc* rep from * to * around. Slst to join rnd.

Rnd 23: Ch3, sk next sc, vshell in next sc *sk next sc, 1dc in next sc, sk next sc, vshell in next sc* rep from * to * around to last 5sc, sk next 2sc, vshell in next sc, sk next 2sc. Slst to join rnd.

Rnd 24: Ch1, 1sc in same st as joining, *7dc in vshell, 1sc in next dc* rep from * to * around. Slst to join rnd. Fasten off and weave in ends.

Follow same instructions as for roses around waist of romper, working roses on rnd 11 of hat.

18–24 months

Rnd 8: *1sc in next 6sc, 2sc in next sc* rep from * to * around. (48sc)

Rnd 9: *1sc in next 7sc, 2sc in next sc* rep from * to * around. (54sc)

Rnd 10: *1sc in next 8sc, 2sc in next sc* rep from * to * around. (60sc)

Rnd 11: *1sc in next 9sc, 2sc in next sc* rep from * to * around. (66sc)

Rnd 12: 1sc in BL of each sc around. (66sc)

Rnd 13: Slst in next sc, ch3, (1dc, ch1, 2dc) in same st, *sk next sc, 1dc in next sc, sk next sc, (2dc, ch1, 2dc) in next sc* rep from * to * around to last 5sc, sk next 2sc, 1dc in next sc, sk next 2sc. Slst to top of ch3 to join. (16 vshells,)

Rnd 14: Slst in next ch1sp, beg vshell, 1fpdc around next dc, *vshell in next ch1sp, 1fpdc around next dc* rep from * to * around. Slst to top of ch3 to join rnd. (16vshells)

Rnds 15–22: Slst in next ch1sp, beg vshell, 1fpdc around next fpdc, *vshell in next ch1sp, 1fpdc around next fpdc* rep from * to * around. Slst to top of ch3 to join rnd. (16vshells)

Rnd 23: Ch1, 1sc in same st as joining, *sk next dc, 1sc in chsp, sk next dc, 1sc in next dc, 1sc in next fpdc, 1sc in next dc* rep from * to * around. Slst to join rnd. (64sc)

Rnd 24: Ch1, 1sc in BL of same st as joining, *2sc in BL next sc, 1sc in BL of next sc* rep from * to * around. Slst to join rnd.

Change to D hook

Rnd 25: With D hook, ch3, sk next sc, vshell in next sc, sk next sc, 1dc in next sc, sk next sc, *vshell in next sc, sk next sc, 1dc in next sc, sk next sc* rep from * to * around. Slst to 3rd ch to join rnd.

Rnd 26: Ch1, 1sc in same st as joining, ch1, *8dc in vshell, ch1, 1sc in next dc, ch1* rep from * to* around. Slst to join rnd. Fasten off and weave in ends.

Follow same instructions as for roses around waist of romper, on rnd 12 of hat.

Hanging Ribbons on Back of Hat
Row 1: With F hook and Chartreuse, ch4, 1dc in 4th ch from hook. Do not turn.

Row 2: Ch3, 1dc in between ch3 and dc from previous rnd.

Rows 3–20: rep row 2. At end of row 20, fasten off leaving a long tail to sew with. Weave tail half way to row 10 and tack ribbon on back of hat on top of roses.

Hanging Ribbons on Back of Romper
Row 1: With F hook and Chartreuse, ch4, 1dc in 4th ch from hook. Do not turn.

Row 2: Ch3, 1dc in between ch3 and dc from previous rnd.

Rows 3–40: rep row 2. At end of row 40, fasten off leaving a long tail to sew with. Weave tail half way to row 20 and tack ribbon on back of romper on top of roses

Ribbon Leaves
make 2
Rnd 1: With F hook and Chartreuse, ch10, 1sc in 2nd ch from hook, 1hdc in next ch, 1dc in next 2ch, 1trc in next ch, 1dc in next 2ch, 1hdc in next ch, 2sc in next ch, ch3, slst in top of last sc, 1sc in same last ch. Now working on opposite side of ch and mirroring your sts, 1hdc in next st, 1dc in next 2sts, 1trc in next st, 1dc in next 2sts, 1hdc in next st. slst in next st to join rnd. Fasten off leaving a tail to sew with. Sew both leaves as shown in pic to top of hanging ribbons. Weave in all ends.

Snail Diaper Bag

Do you take things slow? Or, are you always on the go? With this stylish snail diaper bag you'll be setting the pace and always ready to go anywhere.

Yarn

Cascade Pinwheel 7oz/200g/440yds/400m/#4 medium weight

Colors used in pictures:

Color number 04 / Color name: Easter Eggs x 3 skeins

Cascade 220 Superwash 3.5oz/100g/220yds/200m/#4 medium weight

Colors used in pictures:

Color number 871 / Color name: White x 4yds

Color number 851 / Color name: Lime x 2oz

Color number 849 / Color name: Dark Aqua x 3oz

Color number 825 / Color name: Orange x 1oz

Needle

US G6/4.00mm Susan Bates hook

US H8/5.00mm Susan Bates hook

Yarn needle

Gauge

12sc x 16sc rows = 4"

Also Needed

9mm black safety eyes

Glossary of Abbreviations

st(s) = stitch(es)

slst = slip stitch

ch = chain

yo = yarn over

rnd(s) = round(s)

BL = backloop(s)

sc = single crochet

esc = extended single crochet

rep from * to* = repeat from between the stars

esc = extended single crochet: insert hook in indicated st or row, yo, pull up loop, yo, pull through 1lp on hook, yo, pull through 2lps on hook

BAG
(Note: See Snail Diaper Bag stitches p. 108)

Rnd 1: With H hook and Easter Egg, ch31, 3sc in 2nd ch from hook, 1sc in next 28ch, 3sc in last ch. Now working on opposite side of ch, 1sc in next 28ch. Slst to first sc to join rnd. (62sc). (See Fig 1 on p. 108)

Rnd 2: Ch1, 2sc in same st as joining, 2sc in next 2sc, 1sc in next 28sc, 2sc in next 3sc, 1sc in next 28sc. Slst to join rnd. (68sc)

Rnd 3: Ch1, 2sc in same st as joining, (1sc in next sc, 2sc in next sc) x 2, 1sc in next 29sc, (1sc in next sc, 2sc in next sc) x 3, 1sc in next 28sc. Slst to join rnd. (74sc)

Rnd 4: Ch1, 2sc in same st as joining, (1sc in next 2sc, 2sc in next sc) x 2, 1sc in next 29sc, (1sc in next 2sc, 2sc in next sc) x 3, 1sc in next 29sc. Slst to join rnd. (80sc)

Rnd 5: Ch1, 1sc in the BL in same st as joining, 1sc in BL of each sc around. Slst to join rnd. (80sc)

Rnd 6: Ch1, 1esc in same st as joining, 1esc in each sc around. Slst to join rnd. (80esc)

Rnds 7–32: Ch1, 1esc in same st as joining, 1esc in each esc around. Slst to join rnd. (80esc) At the end of rnd 32, fasten off and weave in ends.

STRAP HANDLE
make 2
Row 1: With H hook and Easter Egg, ch6, 1sc in 2nd ch from hook, 1sc in next 4ch. Turn. (5sc)

Rows 2–150: Ch1, 1sc in each sc across. Turn. (5sc) Fasten off and weave in ends.

Next: hold two straps together and sc in ends of rows around all sides of handle. Fasten off leaving a tail to sew with. Sew one side of strap on inside of bag, starting it on the bottom edge of bag, sewing it in securely. Then go to other side and do the same.

Snail Diaper Bag stitches

(Fig 1) working on opposite side of chain for bottom of bag. (See p. 107.)

(Fig 2) making eyes. (See below and opposite.)

(Fig 3) snail body with no shell on it. (See Face and Body, Row 1, opposite.)

(Fig 4) snail with shell on back. (See opposite, Snail Shell on Back.)

(Fig 5) trim added to shell. (See opposite, row 1, Trim on Shell.)

(Fig 6) finished bag.

SNAIL

First Eye

Rnd 1: With G hook and White, ch2, 6sc in 2nd ch from hook. (6sc). (See Fig 2 above.)

Rnd 2: 1sc in next 6sc. Fasten off White.

Rnd 1: With Lime Green and G hook, attach Lime Green to any sc, 2sc in same st as joining, 1sc in next 2sc, 2sc in next sc, 1sc in next 2sc. Slst to join. Turn. (8sc)

You now are going to work in rows:
Row 1: Ch1, 1sc in next 2sc. Turn. (2sc)

Rows 2–3: Ch1, 1sc in next 2sc. Turn. (2sc) At the end of row 3, fasten off and put aside for now.

Second Eye

Rnd 1: With G hook and White, ch2, 6sc in 2nd ch from hook. (6sc)

Rnd 2: 1sc in next 6sc. Fasten off White. (See Fig 2 opposite.)

Rnd 1: With Lime Green and G hook, attach Lime Green to any sc, 2sc in same st as joining, 1sc in next 2sc, 2sc in next sc, 1sc in next 2sc. Slst to join. Turn. (8sc)

You now are going to work in rows:

Row 1: Ch1, 1sc in next 2sc. Turn. (2sc)

Rows 2–3: Ch1, 1sc in next 2sc. Turn. (2sc)

FACE AND BODY

Row 1: Ch1, keeping second eye in hand, pick up first eye and work 1sc in next 2sc. Turn. (4sc). (See Fig 3 opposite.)

Row 2: Ch1, 2sc in next sc, 1sc in each sc to last sc, 2sc in last sc. Turn. (6sc)

Rows 3–5: Ch1, 2sc in next sc, 1sc in each sc to last sc, 2sc in last sc. Turn. (12sc)

Rows 6–9: Ch1, 1sc in each sc across. Turn. (12sc)

Rows 10–12: Ch1, sc2tog, 1sc in each sc to last 2sc, sc2tog. Turn. (6sc)

Rows 13–45: Ch1, 1sc in each sc across. Turn. (6sc)

Row 46: Ch1, sc2tog, 1sc in next 2sc, sc2tog. Turn. (4sc)

Row 47: Ch1, sc2tog, 1sc in next 2sc. Turn. (3sc)

Row 48: Ch1, sc3tog. Fasten off leaving a long tail to sew with.

Next: push your black eyes into centers of the white circles. Sew all of the Lime Green part of snail to front of bag.

Sew snail face and body to front of bag.

Snail Shell on Back

Note: work all rnds in BL. (See Fig 4, opposite.)

Rnd 1: With Dark Aqua and H hook, ch2, 6sc in 2nd ch from hook. (6sc) Work in continuous rnds.

Rnd 2: 2dc in each sc around. (12dc)

Rnd 3: 2dc in each dc around. (24dc)

Rnd 4: 2dc in each dc around. (48dc)

Rnd 5: 1dc in each dc around. (48dc) Fasten off leaving a tail to sew with.

TRIM ON SHELL

Rnd 1: With Orange and G hook, attach yarn to first unworked FL on shell, (1slst, ch1) in each unworked FL around on rnds 1–5. Fasten off leaving a tail to sew with. Sew Shell on back of body. (See Fig 5, opposite.)

CHANGING PAD

Row 1: With H hook and Easter Egg, ch 31, 1esc in 2nd ch from hook, 1esc in each rem ch across. Turn. (30esc)

Rows 2–54: Ch1, 1esc in each esc across. Turn. (30sc)

You now are going to work in rnds.

Rnd 1: Ch1, 1sc in next 30esc, 1sc in next 54 ends of rows, 1sc in next 30ch, 1sc in next 54 ends of rows. Turn.

Rnds 2–6: Ch1, 1sc in each sc around and at the same time work 3 sc in each corner. Fasten off and weave in ends.

Sunflower Hat

Why tiptoe through the tulips when you could sashay through stunning sunflowers? And your precious blossom will be the most stunning of them all. Adorned in this merino wool sunflower hat, your little sprout will be the centerpiece of the garden. Let your love grow and capture that special moment with a photo that will be treasured for years to come.

Yarn

Cascade Pacific 3.5 oz/100g/213yds/105m/ #4 medium weight

40% Superwash Merino Wool/60% Acrylic

Colors used in pictures:

Color number 13 / Color name: Gold x 1 skein

Color number 30 / Color name: Latte x 1 skein

Cascade Superwash 220 3.5oz/100g/220yds/200m/ #4 medium weight

Colors used in pictures:

Color number 802 / Color name: Green Apple x 2oz

Needle

Yarn Needle

Gauge

I hook = 13dc x 7dc rows = 4"

Glossary of Abbreviations

st(s) = stitch(es)

ch = chain

yo = yarn over hook

slst =slip stitch

sc = single crochet

dc = double crochet

trc = treble crochet

rnd(s) = round(s)

sk = skip

rep from * to* = repeat from between the stars

trc = treble crochet: yo 2 times, insert hook into sc, bring yarn back through, yo, drop of first 2loops, yo, drop off next 2loops, yo, drop off last 2loops.

sctog2 = single crochet together next 2sc

Note: Ch3 counts as first dc

BONNET
Work Rnds 1–3 for all sizes:

Rnd 1: With I hook and Latte, ch3, 11dc in 3nd ch from hook. Slst to join. Turn. (12dc)

Rnd 2: Ch3, 1dc in same st as joining, 2dc in each dc around. Slst to join. Turn. (24dc)

Rnd 3: Ch3, 2dc in next dc, (1dc in next dc, 2dc in next dc) repeat around. Slst to join. Turn. (36dc)

0–3 months 14"circumference
You now are going to work in rows.

Row 1: Ch3, 1dc in next 33dc. Turn. (34dc) leaving the last 2dc unworked for neck opening. (See Fig 1, opposite.)

Rows 2–4: Ch3, 1dc in each dc across. Turn. (34dc)

Row 5: Ch3, 1dc in next 34dc, ch14, skip neck opening and work 1slst in top of ch3. Turn.

You now are going to work in rnds again.

Rnd 1: Ch1, 1sc in each ch and each dc around. Slst to join. (49sc)

Note: next 2 rnds all stitches are worked in the backloops.

Rnd 2: Ch1, 1sc in same st as joining, 1sc in next 2sc, *sc2tog, 1sc in next 3sc* rep from * to * around. Slst to join.

Rnd 3: Ch1, 1sc in each sc around. Slst to join. Fasten off and weave in ends.

Continue on to Neck Trim.

3–6 months 15" circumference
Rnd 4: Ch3, 1dc in next 7dc, 2dc in next dc, *1dc in next 8dc, 2dc in next dc* rep from * to * around. Slst to join. (40dc)

You now are going to work in rows.

Row 1: Ch3, 1dc in next 35dc. Turn. (36dc) leaving the last 4dc unworked for neck opening.

Rows 2–4: Ch3, 1dc in each dc across. Turn. (36dc)

Row 5: Ch3, 1dc in next 36dc, ch14, skip neck opening and work 1slst in top of ch3. Turn.

You now are going to work in rnds again.

Rnd 1: Ch1, 1sc in each ch and each dc around. Slst to join. (51sc)

Note: next 2 rnds all stitches are worked in the backloops.

Rnd 2: Ch1, 1sc in same st as joining, 1sc in next 2sc, *sc2tog, 1sc in next 3sc* rep from * to * around. Slst to join.

Rnd 3: Ch1, 1sc in each sc around. Slst to join. Fasten off and weave in ends. Continue on to Neck Trim.

6–12 months 16" circumference
Rnd 4: Ch3, 1dc in next dc, dc in next dc, *1dc in next 2dc, 2dc in next dc* rep from * to * around. Slst to join. (48dc)

You now are going to work in rows.

Row 1: Ch3, 1dc in next 43dc. Turn. (44dc) leaving the last 4dc unworked for neck opening.

Rows 2–5: Ch3, 1dc in each dc across. Turn. (44dc)

Row 6: Ch3, 1dc in next 44dc, ch14, skip neck opening and work 1slst in top of ch3. Turn.

You now are going to work in rnds again.

Rnd 1: Ch1, 1sc in each ch and each dc around. Slst to join. (59sc)

Note: next 2 rnds all stitches are worked in the backloops.

Rnd 2: Ch1, 1sc in same st as joining, 1sc in next 2sc, *sc2tog, 1sc in next 3sc* rep from * to * around. Slst to join.

Rnd 3: Ch1, 1sc in each sc around. Slst to join. Fasten off and weave in ends. Continue on to Neck Trim.

12–18 months 17" circumference
Rnd 4: Ch3, 1dc in next dc, 2dc in next dc, *1dc in next 2dc, 2dc in next dc* rep from * to * around. Slst to join. Turn. (48dc)

Rnd 5: Ch3, 1dc in next 23dc, 2dc in next dc, 1dc in next 23dc, 2dc in next dc. Slst to join. Turn. (50dc)

You now are going to work in rows.

Row 1: Ch3, 1dc in next 45dc. Turn. (46dc) leaving the last 4dc unworked for neck opening.

Rows 2–6: Ch3, 1dc in each dc across. Turn. (46dc)

Row 7: Ch3, 1dc in next 45dc, ch14, skip neck opening and work 1slst in top of ch3. Turn.

You now are going to work in rnds again.

Rnd 1: Ch1, 1sc in each ch and each dc around. Slst to join. (60sc)

Note: next 2 rnds all stitches are worked in the backloops.

Rnd 2: Ch1, 1sc in same st as joining, 1sc in next 2sc, *sc2tog, 1sc in next 3sc* rep from * to * around. Slst to join.

Rnd 3: Ch1, 1sc in each sc around. Slst to join. Fasten off and weave in ends. Continue on to Neck Trim.

18–24 months 18"circumference
Rnd 4: Ch3, 1dc in next dc, 2dc in next dc, *1dc in next 2dc, 2dc in next dc* rep from * to * around. Slst to join. Turn. (48dc)

Rnd 5: Ch3, 1dc in next 5dc, 2dc in next dc, *1dc in next 6dc, 2dc in next dc* rep from * to * around. Slst to join. Turn. (54dc)

You now are going to work in rows.

Row 1: Ch3, 1dc in next 49dc. Turn. (50dc) leaving the last 4dc unworked for neck opening.

Rows 2–7: Ch3, 1dc in each dc across. Turn. (50dc)

Row 8: Ch3, 1dc in next 50dc, ch14, skip neck opening and work 1slst in top of ch3. Turn.

You now are going to work in rnds again.

Rnd 1: Ch1, 1sc in each ch and each dc around. Slst to join. (65sc)

Note: next 2 rnds all stitches are worked in the backloops.

Rnd 2: Ch1, 1sc in same st as joining, 1sc in next 2sc, *sc2tog, 1sc in next 3sc* rep from * to * around. Slst to join.

Rnd 3: Ch1, 1sc in each sc around. Slst to join. Fasten off and weave in ends. Continue onto Neck Trim.

Sunflower Hat stitches

(Fig 1) forming neck opening. (See opposite, Bonnet, Row 1, all sizes.)

(Fig 2) first row of green on neck. (See p.114.)

(Fig 3) 2nd rnd of green on neck. (See p. 114.)

(Fig 4) front and back rows of Back Petals. (See Rnd 1, p. 114.)

Neck Trim for all sizes

Rnd 1: With I hook and Green Apple, attach yarn to any stitch at neck opening, 2sc in same st as joining, 2sc in each st and end of rows around. Slst to join. (See Fig 2, p. 113.)

Rnd 2: Ch3, 1dc in each sc around. Slst to join. Fasten off and weave in ends. (See Fig 3, p. 113.)

FRONT PETALS

Front row of petals:

Rnd 1: With front of bonnet facing you and with Gold and I hook, attach yarn to any unworked loop on front rnd of unworked loops on bonnet, 1Sc in same st as joining, *(ch3, 2dc, ch3, 1sc) all in same unworked loop, 1sc in each of the next 4 unworked loops* rep from * to* around. Slst to join.

Rnd 2: Ch1, *2sc around the ch3 post, (1hdc, 1dc, 1trc) all in next dc, (1trc, 1dc, 1hdc) all in next dc, 2sc around the ch3 post, 1slst in next sc, skip next sc, 1sc in next sc, skip the next sc, 1slst in next sc* rep from * to* around. Slst to join.

BACK PETALS

Back row of petals:

Rnd 1: Ch1, slst into next row behind the petals, 1sc in same st as joining, 1sc in next 2unworked loops, *(ch5, 2trc, ch5, 1sc) all in same unworked loop, 1sc in each of the next 4 unworked loops* rep from * to* around. Slst to join. (See Fig 4, p. 113.)

Rnd 2: Ch1, 1sc in same st as joining, sk next sc, slst in next sc, *4sc around the ch5 post, (1hdc, 1dc, 1trc) all in next trc, (1trc, 1dc, 1hdc) all in next trc, 4sc around the ch5 post, 1slst in next sc, skip next sc, 1sc in next sc, skip next sc, 1slst in next sc* rep from * to* around. Slst to join. Fasten off leaving a long tail to sew with. Sew front and back petals together, staggering the petals.

Sweet Bonnet and Adorable Bear

What's the buzz? There are no bees in the bonnet and your precious little moppet has been captivated by this cuddly bear! Whether Romeo is spruced up in the classic design or Juliet is adorned in the scalloped edge, either will cherish the comfort and softness of Cascade 220 Superwash wool. Creating the perfect photo prop will 'bearly' take any effort.

Yarn

Cascade 220 Superwash 3.5oz/ 100gram/220yds/200m/
 #4 medium weight

Colors used in pictures:

Color number 871 / Color name: White x 1 skein

Color number 815 / Color name: Black x small amount for face

Needle

US G6/4.00mm Susan Bates hook

Gauge

13vsc rows = 6.5"vsc = 4"

Also Needed

Polyester Fiberfil

Glossary of Abbreviations

st(s) = stitch(es)	tog = together
slst – slip stitich	sk = skip
rnd(s) = rounds	BL = back loop
yo = yarn over	FL = front loop
rep = repeat	chsp = chain space
rem = remaining	ch = chain

sc = single crochet

dc = double crochet

rep from * to * = repeat between the stars

hdc = half double crochet

vsc = v single crochet: (1sc, ch2, 1sc) all in same sc or ch2sp

fpsc = front post single crochet: insert hook from front to back and to front again around the vertical post (upright part) of next st, yo and draw yarn through, yo and draw through last 2 loops on hook to complete fpsc

Finished Sizes

Bear measures approx 9" tall

 0–3 months, 3–6 months, 6–12 months, 12–18 months, 18–24 months

Instructions are written 0–3, other sizes are in parenthesis

The following is an approximate sizing for baby head circumferences.

0–3 months = 14.5", 3–6 months = 15", 6–12 months = 16", 12–18 months = 17", 18–24 months = 20"

When trying to decide which size to make for your baby. I recommend making the one closest to the baby's head circumference. Not their age.

BONNET

Row 1: With White, ch49 (52, 55, 58, 61), 1sc in 2nd ch from hook, 1sc in each rem ch. Turn. (48, 51, 54, 57, 60sc)

Row 2: Ch 1, 1sc in first sc, *vsc, sk next 2sc* rep from * to * across to last 2sc, vsc, 1sc in last sc. Turn. (16, 17, 18, 19, 20vsc)

Rows 3–15 (3–16, 3–17, 3–18, 3–19): Ch1, 1sc in first sc, vsc in each ch2sp across to last sc, 1sc in last sc. Turn. (16, 17, 18, 19, 20vsc). (See Figs 1 and 2, p. 120.)

Or work rows until hat measures approx
0–3 months = 4.5"
3–6 months = 4.75"
6–12 months = 5"
12–18 months = 5.25"
18–24 months = 5.5"

Next: Ch1, 1sc in each end of row on side A.
Ch1, 1sc in each st on starting ch on side B.
Then: Fold last row of sc in half, side B, (creating back of hat). Holding last sc to first sc, sc together the two sides working through both thicknesses. Turn. (See Fig 3, p.120.)

Ch1, slst in each sc across back to opening of bonnet. Ch1. (See Fig 4 p.120.)

Stitches on back of hat are on the inside of hat, so now turn hat inside out, this brings you to the middle of the neck side of the hat or Side C, 1sc in each end of rows on left side of bonnet, (neck edge made). Turn.

Row 1: Ch1, 1sc in each sc across neck edge. (Sides A and C) Turn. (See Fig 5, p. 120.)

Row 2: Ch1, 1sc in each sc across neck edge. Do not turn. See Fig 5.

Next: Ch1, 1sc in each sc and in each ch2sp across Side D. Turn

To make a plain front bonnet

Row 1: Ch1, 1sc in each sc across. Turn.

Row 2: Ch51, (first tie) 1sc in 5th ch from hook, *ch5, sk next 4ch, 1sc in next ch* rep across ch, 1slst in first sc, 1sc in each sc across to other side of bonnet, (2nd tie). Ch51, 1sc in 5th ch from hook, *ch5, sk next 4ch, 1sc in next ch* rep across chains, slst in last st. Fasten off and weave in all ends.

To make a scallop front bonnet

Row 1: Ch1, 1fpsc in each sc across front. Turn. (See Fig 6, p. 120.)

Row 2: (first tie) ch51, 1sc in 5th ch from hook, *ch5, sk next 4ch, 1sc in next ch* rep from * to * across ch, 1slst in first sc, Now working under the front 2 loops, in the stitches that are closest to you, *sk next 2sts, 7dc in next st, sk next 2sts, 1sc in next sc* rep from * to * across to other side of front of bonnet. (2nd tie) ch51, 1sc in 5th ch from hook, *ch5, sk next 4ch, 1sc in next ch* rep from * to * across chain. Fasten off and weave in ends. (See Fig 7, p.120.)

BEAR
Note: make arms and legs first before body of bear.

ARMS
Rnd 1: With G hook and White, make a magic circle (see p. 4), 6sc inside magic circle. Pull loop closed. (6sc)

Rnd 2: 2sc in each sc around. (12sc)

Rnds 3–8: 1sc in each sc around. (12sc)

Rnd 9: (sc tog the next 2sc) x 6

Row 1: Stuff arms, fold arm in half and sc tog the top 3sc to close the arm. Fasten off and weave in ends. Make 2.

FEET
Rnd 1: With G hook and White, ch5, 2sc in 2nd ch from hook, 1sc in next 2ch, 5sc in last ch. Now working on opposite side of ch, 1sc in next 2ch, 1sc in same ch as beg. Slst to join. Ch1. (12sc)

Rnd 2: 2sc in same st as joining, 2sc in next sc, 1sc in next 2sc, 2sc in each of the next 5sc, 1sc in next 2sc, 2sc in last sc. (20sc)

Rnd 3: 1sc in same st as joining, 1sc in each sc around. Slst to join. Ch1. (20sc)

Rnd 4: 1sc in same st as joining, 1sc in next 6sc, (sc tog the next 2sc, 1sc in next sc) 4 times, 1sc in last sc. Slst to join. Ch1. (16sc)

Rnd 5: 1sc in same st as joining, 1sc in next 6sc, (sc tog the next 2sc) 4 times, 1sc in last sc. Slst to join. Ch1. (12sc)

Sweet Bonnet stitches

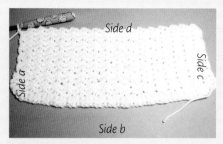

(Fig 1) all 4 sides A, B, C, D.

(Fig 2) bonnet 2 crochet down side A. (See Bonnet first instructions, p.119.)

(Fig 3) fold side B in half and crochet together.

(Fig 4) slst back to front of bonnet. (See instructions, p.119.)

(Fig 5) sc on back of neck. (See Row 1, Bonnet, p.119.)

(Fig 6) fpsc across front of bonnet for girls. (See Row 1, scallop trim, p.119.)

(Fig 7) scallops trim edge for girls. (See Row 2, p.119.)

(Fig 8) front of girl bonnet.

Rnds 6–10: 1sc in same st as joining, 1sc in each sc around. Slst to join. Ch1. (12sc) Stuff foot and leg lightly.

Row 1: Fold rnd 10 in half so that the foot is facing front. Working through both thicknesses, 1sc in next 6sc. Closing the top of the leg. Fasten off weaving in ends. Make 2.

BEAR HEAD AND BODY

Rnd 1: With G hook and White, make a magic circle (see p. 4), 6sc inside loop. (6sc) Continue in a spiral fashion, using a place marker if desired.

Rnd 2: 2sc in each sc around. (12sc)

Rnd 3: 2sc in next sc, all in next FL work, (1hdc, 3dc, 1hdc) (1st ear), 2sc in next 5sc, all in next FL work, (1hdc, 3dc, 1hdc) (2nd ear), 2sc in next 5sc. (22sts)

Rnd 4: 1sc in next 2sc, 2sc in BL behind 1st ear, 1sc in next 10sc, 2sc in BL behind 2nd ear, 1sc in next 10sc. (24sc)

Rnds 5–7: 1sc in each sc around. (24sc)

Rnd 8: *1sc in next 3sc, 2sc next sc* rep from * to * around. (30sc)

Rnds 9–11: 1sc in each sc around. (30sc)

Start to stuff head

Rnd 16: dec with slst 15 times. (15sc)

Rnd 17: dec with slst 7 times, 1sc in last sc. (8sts) Finish stuffing head.

Rnd 18: 3sc in each st around. (24sc)

Rnd 19: 1sc in next 7sc, next hold 3sc of arm to next 3sc on body, working through both thicknesses, 1sc in next 3sc, 1sc in next 9sc, next hold 3sc of arm to next 3sc on body, working through both thicknesses, 1sc in next 3sc, 1sc in last 2sc. (24sc)

Rnd 20: *1sc in next 3sc, 2sc in next sc* rep from * to * around. (30sc)

Rnds 21–29: 1sc in each sc around. (30sc)

Rnd 30: *1sc in next 3sc, sc tog the next 2sc* rep from * to * around. (24sc)

Stuff body.

Row 1: 1sc in next 5sc, fold body flat and and sc together the two sides to close the bottom. Turn. (12sc)

Next: Ch1, hold 1st foot up to next 6sc, working through both thicknesses, 1sc in next 6sc, making sure that the toes are facing down, so when you flip them up, the toes will be facing forward. Pick up 2nd foot and repeat as for first foot. Fasten off and weave in ends.

EARS
make 2
Row 1: With G hook and White, make a magic circle (see p. 4), 6sc inside loop, pull loop closed, but not tight. You want to form a half circle. (6sc) Turn.

Row 2: *2sc in first sc, 1sc in next sc* rep from * to * one more time, 2 sc in last sc. Fasten off, leaving a tail to sew with. Attach ears to top of head.

MUZZLE
Rnd 1: With G hook and White, ch5, 3sc in 2nd ch from hook, 1sc in next 2ch, 3sc in last ch. Now working on opposite side of ch, 1sc in next 2ch. Slst to join rnd. (10sc)

Rnd 2: Ch1, 1sc in same st as joining, 1sc in each sc around. Slst to join rnd. (10sc) Fasten off, leaving a tail to sew with. Attach snout to front of face.

With Black, embroider eye, nose and mouth as in the pictures with straight stitch and yarn needle.

Princess Rose Tulle Dress

Hear ye, hear ye: come one, come all and see the dress that's fit for a queen, but made for the little princess in your life. Fun and fanciful, this imaginative creation will have heads turning and asking about a royal wedding. The possibilities are endless: tea parties, dances, christenings or Halloween – create a fairytale that will be told for years to come.

Yarn

Cascade 220 Superwash/3.5oz/100gr/220yds/200m/ #4 medium weight

Colors used in pictures:

Color number 836 / Color name: Pink Ice x 1 skein

Color number 851 / Color name: Lime x 1 skein

Needle

US G6/4.00mm Susan Bates hook

Yarn needle

Materials needed for Tulle dress

Crochet Headband stretch trim 1¾" wide x 2yds long

200yds of desired color tulle (spools of 3" x 100yds) cut into 2.5' long strips

White satin ribbon x 1" wide x about 2' long

(Note: See p. 128 Resources – should you prefer to order the tulle dress and then add the crochet roses)

Glossary of Abbreviations

st(s) = stitch(es)

sk = skip

chsp = chain space

slst = slip stitch

ch = chain

sc = single crochet

dc = double crochet

hdc = half double crochet

rep from * to * = repeat between the stars

Suggested Headband Sizes

0–3 months = 17"

3–6 months = 18"

6–12 months = 19"

12–18 months = 20"

18–24 months = 21"

SMALL ROSES

make 30

Row 1: With G hook and Pink Ice, ch10, 2sc in 2nd ch from hook, 2sc in next 2ch, 2hdc in next 3ch, 3dc in next 3ch. Fasten off leaving a tail to sew with. Roll stitches into a rose shape and draw some yarn through bottom of roll stitches to hold them into a rose shape. Leave tail to sew to tulle skirt. (See Figs 1, 2, and 3, below.)

SMALL LEAVES

make 30

Rnd 1: With G hook and Lime ch6, 1sc in 2nd ch from hook, 1hdc in next ch, 1dc in next ch, 1hdc in next ch, 1sc in last ch, ch3, slst in 2nd ch from hook, 1sc in next ch, slst in top of sc. Now working on opposite side of leaf, 1hdc in next ch, 1dc in next ch, 1hdc in next ch, slst to first st to join. Fasten off leaving to tail to sew with. Sew leaf onto bottom of small roses.

Sew roses onto tulle anywhere desired.

LARGE ROSES

make 3

Row 1: With G hook and Pink Ice, ch31, 1dc in 5th ch from hook (counts as 1dc and ch2) *ch2, sk next ch, 1dc in next ch* rep from * to * across. Turn (14ch2sps). (See Figs 4 and 5, below.)

Row 2: Slst into first dc, 5dc in next ch2sp, 1slst in next dc, 5dc in next ch2sp, 1slst in next dc, 5dc in next ch2sp, (1slst in next dc, 6dc in next ch2sp) x 4, (1slst in next dc, 7dc in next ch2sp) x 3, (1slst in next dc, 8dc in next ch2sp) x 4, 1slst in last dc.

Fasten off leaving a tail to sew with. Roll stitches into a rose shape. Run a few stitches through the bottom to hold stitches into a rose shape. Leave tail to sew to front of dress.

Rose stitches

(Fig 1) foundation row.

(Fig 2) crochet 5dc around 1st dc for Small Rose.

(Fig 3) petal construction for Small Rose.

(Fig 4) assembly for Large Rose.

(Fig 5) finished petals of Large Rose.

(Fig 6) sewn onto bodice with leaves.

LARGE LEAVES

make 3. (See Figs 7, 8, and 9, below)

Rnd 1: With G hook and Lime, ch9, 1sc in 2nd ch from hook, 1hdc in next 2ch, 1dc in next 2ch, 1hdc in next 2ch, 1sc in last ch, ch4, 1slst in 2nd ch from hook, 1slst in next ch, 1sc in next ch, 1sc in same st as last ch. Now working on opposite side of leaf, 1hdc in next 2ch, 1dc in next 2ch, 1sc in last ch. Slst to join rnd. Fasten off leaving a tail to sew with. Sew green leaf on back of flower.

Sew flower on the front of the dress.

Large rose and leaf stitches

(Fig 7) leaf. See Rnd 1, above.

(Fig 8) leaf construction. See Rnd 1, above.

(Fig 9) finished rose

Acknowledgements

First I would like to thank all the mom's and babies that donated their time to helping us get all these wonderful pictures for this book. I appreciate all of you!

Also I need to thank Tara's mom, Loretta Watson, from Berkley, MA, for once again letting us use her beautiful secret garden to get so many of these shots. Your yard is beautiful and made our pictures so perfect.

http//www.freshfacephotos.com

I would like to thank all the people that helped me so much with the making of this book.

First I would like to thank my niece Jill Silvia from Bridgewater, MA. Without your help over the last year I would not of been able to get all of this done. Thank you so much for all your yarn unsnarling, your yarn sortings, your filing and keeping all my pictures and patterns in order. And thank you so much for your delightful blurbs that bring out the character and fun in each of my creations. You truly have a gift for words.

Next I would like to thank Bonnie Quindley from Forestdale, MA for all of her hard work and dedication to working side by side with me for the first year of this book.

I also want to thank Bonnie for making those adorable Peony Tulle Dresses for me to sew my lovely roses on to.

I need to thank my wonderful husband for once again being so patient with me during the making of this book.

I also would like to thank the Cascade Yarn Co for all of their wonderful yarns that I was able to work with.

And also I need to thank Jen Heinlen from Sage Yarns. Thank you Jen for helping me with some yarns at the beginning of this journey.

And a big thanks to Jo Bryant and Sellers Publishing for giving me this wonderful opportunity to make another book once again.

Clay hooks were made by Jennifer Wheeler Ellingwood dba Day By Day Crochet

Yarns were donated by *www.cascadeyarns.com*

Some Yarns were used from *www.sageyarns.com*

I would like to give a big special thanks to all the ladies that helped test my patterns.

A big, big thank you to Judy Dake-Finder for helping me do the final tests on all of the patterns.
Judy Dake-Finder from Fairfield, Idaho dba Camas Creations
Audrey Warnecke from Clearwater FL
Beth Massog from Sauk Centre, Minnesota dba Heavenly Handmade Crochet by Beth
Carol Rupprecht from Wilson, North Carolina dba Sweet Potato Crochet Creations
Carmen Ace Johnson
Celyn Collins from Highland IL, dba Celyn's Creations
Dave-Sheila Overturf from Mcleansboro IL dba SissyAnnes Stamps & Stitches
Debby Tumillo from Dacula, Georgia dba Fozybear's Cottage Custom Crochet
Elizabeth Schultz from West Bloomfield, Michigan
Emily Moore Welchman from Charlotte, NC dba My Lil Roo
Jackie Jones from Graham WA dba Urban Hookin
Jennifer Hatch from Superior Wisconsin dba Hatched With Love
Jennifer Lucas from Chatham VA, dba Two Ginger Gypsies
Jennifer Mullin from Asheboro North Carolina
Jessica Gillispie from Bellevue NE dba Jour Jeana Designs
Kendra McGill-Evans from Roanoke Rapids , NC
Lindsey Stippelhoff from Phoneix AZ. Dba Mama Mae Crochet
Lizzie from Dayton, OH dba Lizzie's Lovlies
Malonie Ellingson from Gillette, WY
Martha Shaw from Lexington NC, dba Martha's Crochet World
Michelle Wulf from Anchorage Alaska dba Magic Mommy's Yarning
Nicole Doing is originally from Apple Valley, CA , but currently in Quantico, VA (hubby is in the Marine Corps)
Rachel Ramirez Corneglio from Utica, IL dba The Country Hooker
Rebecca Goldsmith from Aberdeen MD dba Desert Diamond Crochet
Sarah Tompkins from Nekoosa Wisconsin
Steff Walker from Canada dba Steff's Simple Stitches
Susan Higbe from Gig Harbor, WA dba Tiger Lilies Creations
Tiffany Gendron from Burlington NJ dba Create-Tiff Crafts and More

Resources

The tulle dresses can be purchased from Hatched With Love www.facebook.com/hatchedwithlove Hatchedfromjenwithlove@gmail.com

Roses not included. You will make the roses (Note: See p. 124)